American Lives 2

Readings and Language Activities

Gail Feinstein Forman
Developmental Reading and English Language Instructor
San Diego City College

New Readers Press

For Tatiana, Zarina, Darya, and Nik—who brought love from far away

The author and New Readers Press have used all reasonable skill and care to ensure that the historical information presented in this book is accurate. A list of the references consulted and the notes identifying the sources of quotations appears on pages 109–112.

American Lives: Readings and Language Activities, Book 2
ISBN 978-1-56420-436-3

Copyright © 2005 New Readers Press
New Readers Press
ProLiteracy's Publishing Division
104 Marcellus Street, Syracuse, New York 13204
www.newreaderspress.com

Printed in the United States of America
9 8 7 6 5

Proceeds from the sale of New Readers Press materials support professional development, training, and technical assistance programs of ProLiteracy that benefit local literacy programs in the U.S. and around the globe.

Acquisitions Editor: Paula L. Schlusberg
Content Editor: Judi Lauber
Design and Production Manager: Andrea Woodbury
Photo Illustrations: Brian Quoss
Illustrations: Carolyn Boehmer, Amy Simons
Production Specialist: Amy Simons, Jeffrey R. Smith
Cover Design: Kimbrly Koennecke

Contents

Anne Bradstreet

"If we had no winter, the spring would not be so pleasant."

—Anne Bradstreet[1]

Pre-Reading Questions

1. Read the words under the title. What do you think that they mean? Could they apply to someone who moves to a new country? If yes, how?

2. Poetry expresses thoughts and feelings. Do you think that poetry is important? Why or why not?

Reading Preview

Anne Bradstreet was America's first published poet. She wrote about life in early America. She also wrote about her love for her family and her faith in God.

Anne Bradstreet

Anne Bradstreet was one of the early British colonists in America. She was also America's first published poet. Her poems show that she was well educated and loved her family. But most of all, they show that she had deep faith. Bradstreet believed strongly in the power of God.

Anne Bradstreet was born in 1612 in Northampton, England. Her family was prosperous. Her father, Thomas Dudley, worked for the Earl of Lincoln. He managed the earl's property and lived there with his family. The earl had a large home library. Anne spent hours there, reading and studying. She also studied with private tutors.

In 1628, at age 16, Anne Dudley married Simon Bradstreet. The Dudleys and the Bradstreets were Puritans. The Puritans wanted to change the Church of England. They thought that Britain should follow the Bible more closely. Most British people had different beliefs. For that reason, sometimes the British government mistreated the Puritans.

The Puritans wanted freedom for their beliefs. A group of them decided to build a new life in America. The British king gave them permission to settle in Massachusetts. They planned to go to the village of Salem. Thomas Dudley was one of the group's leaders. His family, including Anne and Simon Bradstreet, decided to go with him.

Bradstreet and her family left Britain in April 1630. The trip across the Atlantic Ocean was dangerous. It took more than two months. The Puritans were often cold and seasick. They faced storms in their tiny ship.

When they arrived in Salem, a hard winter was ending. At least 80 colonists were dead. Many others were sick, and they had very little food. Bradstreet's group decided not to settle there.

Instead, they started a new settlement—Cambridge. It was better than Salem, but life was still hard. They had to build houses and plant crops for food. The winters were cold and harsh, and the summers were very hot. Bradstreet was sick often, and she missed life in Britain. Her earliest poems are from this time. She wrote about her thoughts and feelings.

She believed that God wanted her to be in America. She tried to accept God's will.

The Puritans worked hard. By 1634, Cambridge was growing and prosperous. In fact, it was getting crowded. Some families, including the Bradstreets, moved to a new settlement at Ipswich. By this time, Simon Bradstreet was a leader in the colony of Massachusetts. He often had to leave home on colony business.

Anne Bradstreet was lonely then. She turned to her poetry. She wrote beautiful love poems. Her poems said that she missed her husband. She called him "my dear, my joy, my only love"[2] and "the man more lov'd than life."[3] These poems were unusual. In the 1600s, most poets didn't show feelings so clearly.

Bradstreet kept her poetry private. She shared it only with family. Puritans believed that women should not express their thoughts and feelings. They often punished women who spoke in public. But Bradstreet's brother-in-law, John Woodbridge, thought that her poems were good. He wanted more people to read them. He took some of them to Britain and published them in 1650. The book was called *The Tenth Muse.* Many people read it in Britain.

In America, Bradstreet's life continued as usual. She was still sickly and often ill. But she raised eight children. One of her poems was about her children. She said that she missed them when they grew up and left home.

In 1666, the family was living in Andover. One night, their house burned. They lost all their possessions. Bradstreet's papers were destroyed. She wrote a sad poem about the fire. She was trying to accept it as God's will.

In her later years, Bradstreet suffered more and more from sickness. In 1669, she wrote a poem called "As Weary Pilgrim Now at Rest." It said that she was tired of Earth and longed for heaven. She died in 1672. A second book of her poems was published after she died.

Bradstreet is remembered as America's first published poet. Her poems still tell us about life in the early American colonies and her own thoughts and feelings.

Comprehension

Check the correct answer.

1. In Britain, Anne Bradstreet's life

    _____ a. was comfortable.

    _____ b. was difficult.

2. When she was young, Bradstreet

    _____ a. got a good education.

    _____ b. did not get much education.

3. The Puritans left Britain

    _____ a. to have freedom for their beliefs.

    _____ b. to become prosperous.

4. When the Puritans arrived in America,

    _____ a. it was easy to set up a new colony.

    _____ b. there were many problems to solve.

5. Bradstreet wrote poetry about

    _____ a. her life in Britain.

    _____ b. her husband and family.

6. Bradstreet's brother-in-law

    _____ a. never saw her poetry.

    _____ b. published her poetry.

7. When bad things happened, Bradstreet

    _____ a. became angry.

    _____ b. tried to accept God's will.

Bradstreet wrote often about loss. She said that earthly joys don't last. If they did, she asked, "Who would look for heavenly?"[4]

Sequence

Work with a partner. Number the events in the correct order.

_____ The Bradstreet family's house burns.

_____ Bradstreet's husband becomes a leader in Cambridge.

_____ John Woodbridge publishes Bradstreet's poetry in Britain.

_____ Anne Dudley marries Simon Bradstreet.

_____ Bradstreet leaves Britain for America.

Vocabulary

Look at these words from the reading. Put a check next to words that you know. Underline words that you don't know yet. Find the words in the reading. Try to guess their meanings.

faith	longed	possessions	settlement
harsh	mistreated	prosperous	sickly

Use the words to fill in the blanks in the sentences.

1. Bradstreet had strong _____ in God.

2. The Puritans worked hard, and their colony became _____.

3. The British government _____ the Puritans.

4. The Puritans built a new _____—Cambridge.

5. The climate in Massachusetts was _____.

6. Bradstreet was _____ and often became ill.

7. Bradstreet's family lost all their _____ in a fire.

8. Bradstreet _____ to see her husband when he was away.

Reading a Map

Physical maps show features of the land and water. **Political maps** show borders between countries, states, or other political regions. **Historical maps** show features from the past. Some maps, like this one, combine all three types. It shows physical features and settlements in North America during the 17th century. It also shows modern political regions—the states.

Some Early British Settlements

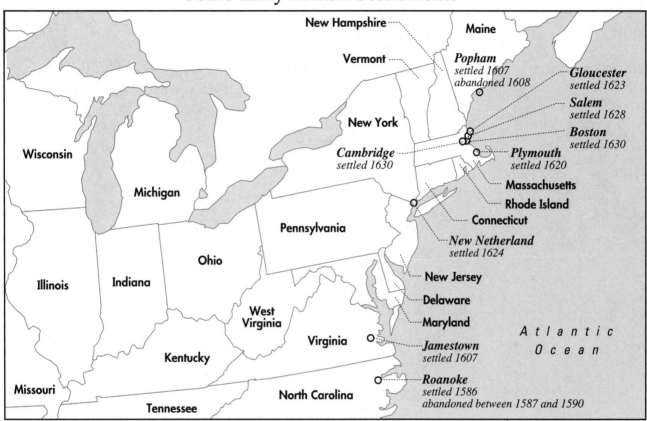

Answer the questions. Use information from the map.

1. Which settlement was the earliest? _____

2. Which settlements failed and were abandoned? _____

_____

3. Which state had the most settlements? _____

4. In which state were Boston and Salem? _____

5. Why were these early settlements on the east coast? _____

_____

Do you have a favorite poem? What is it? What do you like about it?

Connecting Today and Yesterday

1. Bradstreet missed her life in Britain. But she made a new life in America. Did you ever feel homesick? What did you do?

2. Puritan women did not express their opinions in public. How do women writers express their opinions today? Explain.

Group Activity

What do you know about early colonies in America? Find books or pictures that show life then. Bring them to your group. Imagine that you live at that time. Answer the questions.

1. What clothes do you wear?

2. What kind of house do you live in?

3. What kind of job do you have?

4. What do you study in school?

5. What is your family like?

Class Discussion

1. The Puritans had many difficulties in their new life. Why did they stay in America?

2. Why did the British government mistreat the Puritans?

3. John Woodbridge published Bradstreet's poetry. It is possible that he didn't have her permission. If that is true, did he do the right thing? Why or why not?

Reflections

1. What was the most interesting thing that you read in this lesson?

2. How can you learn more about Anne Bradstreet or life in early America?

Samuel Adams

"We love our cup of tea full well, but love our freedom more."

—*popular song in America in the 1700s*[1]

Pre-Reading Questions

1. Read the words under the title. What do you think that they mean?

2. What was the Boston Tea Party? Why did it happen?

Reading Preview

Samuel Adams wanted to live in a free country. He was a leader in the fight for American independence.

Samuel Adams

Samuel Adams came from a political family. His father was active in Boston politics. His cousin, John Adams, was a leader in Massachusetts. Later, John Adams was president of the United States. Samuel Adams helped lead the fight for American independence.

Adams was born in Boston, Massachusetts, in 1722. When he was just 14 years old, he started attending Harvard University. His father wanted him to be a minister. But Adams was interested in politics.

After college, Adams worked for a businessman. But his boss fired him. He thought that Adams wasn't good at business. Then Adams tried to run his own business. The business failed.

In 1756, he became a tax collector. He wasn't good at handling money. But he met many people in his work. He got along well with them. These friendships made him popular. In 1765, he was elected to the Massachusetts government.

At this time, Britain controlled the American colonies. Britain needed more money. So it put taxes on the colonies. In 1765, Britain passed the Stamp Act. This law taxed all papers, including newspapers and legal papers. Adams said that this tax took away colonists' rights. He said that Britain shouldn't tax the colonies. Soon Adams was a leader in the fight against British taxes.

Many colonists were angry about the stamp tax. Adams helped organize them. The groups called themselves Sons of Liberty. The groups tried to convince other colonists not to buy British goods.

Adams spoke out strongly against the stamp tax. The Sons of Liberty in Boston wanted to take action. In August 1765, some of them gathered a mob. The mob threatened and chased tax officials. They robbed houses and broke furniture. And they almost destroyed the house of Thomas Hutchinson. Hutchinson was governor of Massachusetts. These events made tax officials afraid. Many quit their jobs.

Adams didn't tell the Sons of Liberty to use violence. But some people thought that his speeches and writings were too strong. They said that such strong words caused the violence.

Britain ended the stamp tax in 1766. But soon it passed more tax laws. Again, Adams wrote and spoke against these taxes. In 1772, Boston formed the Massachusetts Committee of Correspondence. Adams led the effort. This group sent out political news and ideas. It helped unite people against British taxes.

Then in 1773, Britain passed the Tea Act. Under this law, the British East India Company could sell tea cheaply to the colonies. There was a tax on the tea. This law hurt other tea sellers. And colonists were still angry about British taxes.

Adams and the Sons of Liberty planned a dramatic action. On the night of December 16, 1773, in Boston, a large group of colonists dressed like Native Americans. They boarded three British ships in the harbor. The ships were carrying a cargo of tea. The protestors threw all the tea into Boston Harbor. The tea was worth nearly 10,000 British pounds.

News of this action went around the world. It was called the Boston Tea Party. Britain was angry. In 1774, it closed Boston Harbor. And it took away the government of Massachusetts. Britain told the colonists to pay for the tea. But the colonists refused.

The colonists had a meeting in Philadelphia. People from 12 of the 13 colonies attended the meeting. They discussed their problems. They agreed not to buy British goods.

But Britain continued to try to control the colonies. Fighting broke out in 1775. It was the start of the American Revolution. Colonists met again. In 1776, they talked about becoming a separate nation.

Before the colonists agreed to declare independence, some were unsure. The British could hang them as traitors. Adams gave a speech. He helped convince the colonists to declare independence.

After the Revolution, Adams had several political jobs. He was lieutenant governor of Massachusetts for four years. Later, he was governor of Massachusetts. He also helped write the Massachusetts constitution.

He died on October 2, 1803. Americans remember Samuel Adams because he was not afraid to fight for freedom.

"If I have a wish . . . it is that these American states may never cease to be free and independent." [Cease to be means "stop being."]

—Samuel Adams[2]

Comprehension

Complete the sentences. Use information from the reading.

1. When Adams tried to work in business, _____ *not good for him* _____

   _____ .

2. Adams said that the Stamp Act _____ *took away colonists rights* _____

   _____ .

3. The Sons of Liberty were _____ *do not buy British goods* _____ *fight taxation* _____

   _____ .

4. The Boston Tea Party happened because _____ *tax on tea* _____

   _____ .

5. The Massachusetts Committee of Correspondence was important because

   _____ *helped unite colonists against British taxes* _____

   _____ .

6. Before the colonists declared independence, they worried that

   _____ *unsure be hung* _____

   _____ .

7. After the American Revolution, Adams _____

   _____ .

   lt. gov. gov of Mass.

Fact or Opinion

Work with a partner. Decide if each sentence is a fact or an opinion. Then write *F* for *fact* or *O* for *opinion* in front of each sentence.

_____ 1. Samuel Adams was not a good businessman.

_____ 2. Britain made a mistake when it taxed the colonies.

_____ 3. Samuel Adams worked in politics.

_____ 4. The Sons of Liberty had to use violence.

Vocabulary

Look at these words from the reading. Put a check next to words that you know. Underline words that you don't know yet. Find the words in the reading. Try to guess their meanings.

cargo	dramatic	pass	traitor
declare	mob	rights	unite

Match each word with its definition.

_____ 1. pass   a. an enemy of one's own country

_____ 2. rights   b. entertaining and exciting, like theater

_____ 3. mob   c. to make into a law

_____ 4. unite   d. to say formally in public

_____ 5. dramatic   e. to bring together

_____ 6. cargo   f. freedoms

_____ 7. declare   g. things carried on a ship or other vehicle

_____ 8. traitor   h. an unorganized, sometimes violent crowd

Reading a Chart

A chart is a useful way to organize facts.

Famous Sons of Liberty

Name	Job	Born	Died	Known for
John Hancock	merchant	1737	1793	• helped lead the fight against British taxes • was the first person to sign the Declaration of Independence
Paul Revere	silversmith	1734	1818	• threw tea into Boston Harbor • brought news of British actions from town to town
Haym Salomon	businessman	1740	1785	• got loans from Holland and France to help pay for the Revolution

Answer the questions. Use information from the chart.

1. What was Paul Revere's job? _____

   _____

2. Why was Paul Revere important? _____

   _____

3. What is John Hancock known for? _____

   _____

4. What did Haym Salomon do for a living? _____

   _____

5. What did Haym Salomon do in the Revolution? _____

   _____

6. Which of these men helped in the American Revolution? _____

   _____

Connecting Today and Yesterday

1. Britain and the American colonies were 3,000 miles apart. Do you think this distance made problems? Does this type of situation exist anywhere today?

2. American colonists thought that British taxes were unfair. Is the U.S. tax system fair or unfair? Explain your opinion.

Group Activity

In your group, make a list of three problems that a new country has. Then write one solution for each problem.

Problem	Solution
1. _____	1. _____
2. _____	2. _____
3. _____	3. _____

Share your group's answers with other groups. How many answers are the same? How many are different? Which problem is most important to solve?

Class Discussion

1. The Sons of Liberty used violence. Was that a good idea? Why or why not?

2. Adams was good at making friends. These friendships helped him succeed in politics. What is more important in a job—the work you do, or how you get along with people? Is the answer different for different jobs?

3. Was Samuel Adams a good leader? Why or why not?

Reflections

1. What was the most interesting thing that you read in this lesson?

2. Can you use anything from Samuel Adams's story in your own life? Explain.

Samuel Adams is sometimes called the father of American independence.

Is that a good nickname for him? Why or why not?

Benjamin Franklin

"Early to bed and early to rise, makes a man healthy, wealthy, and wise."

—Benjamin Franklin[1]

Pre-Reading Questions

1. Read the words under the title. What do you think that they mean?

2. Do you know more advice like this? What is it?

Reading Preview

Benjamin Franklin was a famous scientist and politician. He helped make the new United States.

Benjamin Franklin

Benjamin Franklin had many talents. He was a famous scientist. He was a successful businessman. And he was a leader in the American Revolution. His ideas helped to build the new nation.

Franklin was born in Boston in 1706. At age 12, he started working in the print shop of his brother James. Franklin liked the newspaper business. But he didn't like the conservative life in Boston.

Franklin had a good sense of humor. He wrote some funny articles. He signed a false name, and James printed them. When James found out who really wrote them, he became angry. Franklin quarreled with James often. At age 17, Franklin left Boston. He moved to Philadelphia. He liked Philadelphia better. It was an exciting, modern city.

Franklin opened his own print shop in Philadelphia in 1728. He published a newspaper called *The Philadelphia Gazette.* Franklin didn't want anyone to control information. He believed that a free press was important for a free society. So his newspaper printed many different ideas. He also wrote a booklet called *Poor Richard's Almanac.* His shop published it yearly from 1733 to 1758. It gave useful information about the weather and farming. It also contained advice for every day.

Franklin worked hard, and his business was successful. In 1748, he was able to retire. Then he could spend more time on science and inventing.

Franklin was a world-famous scientist. He was best known for his work with electricity. He proved that lightning was electricity. He also invented many useful devices. He was the first person to make eyeglasses with bifocal, or two-part, lenses.

Franklin believed that society should be free and tolerant, or open-minded. He thought that freedom of religion was especially important. In Philadelphia, he helped raise money to build a large religious center. Any religious group in Philadelphia could use it. He also gave money to build places of worship for many different religions.

Franklin was an honest man. He had a son with a woman who was not his wife. He didn't try to hide it. He gave money to take care of the child. And he was not afraid to change his mind. When he was young, Franklin owned slaves. But in 1787, he became president of the Pennsylvania Society for Promoting the Abolition of Slavery. This group worked to end slavery.

Before the American Revolution, Franklin spent many years in London. He argued for the rights of the American colonists. At the time, colonists were angry about British taxes. Britain put a tax on tea in 1773. In Boston, some colonists threw hundreds of chests of tea into the harbor. The British became angry. Franklin wanted to keep peace but still support the colonists. He asked Britain to end the tax, and he would pay for the tea himself. The British refused.

In April 1775, the American Revolution began. The colonies had a special meeting—called the Second Continental Congress—to deal with the emergency. Franklin was a member of the Congress. In 1776, he helped write the Declaration of Independence. His words and ideas helped make the United States a free country.

To win the war against Britain, the United States needed more soldiers and money. So late in 1776, Franklin went to France. He asked France to help. Britain and France were enemies. The French took a long time to decide. But finally, they gave money to the United States. They also sent 44,000 French troops.

Franklin stayed in France for several years. While he was there, he helped write the Treaty of Paris. This document, or official paper, ended the American Revolution in 1783.

In 1787, at age 80, Franklin helped write the U.S. Constitution. This document divided power between the states and the federal government. This was a new kind of government.

Franklin died in 1790. People from all over the country wanted to honor him. More than 20,000 people went to his funeral. It was the largest funeral in America up to that time.

Comprehension

Check the correct answer.

1. Franklin left Boston because

   _____ a. he didn't like working in a print shop.

   _____ b. he didn't like Boston.

2. *The Philadelphia Gazette* printed

   _____ a. only Franklin's opinion.

   _____ b. many opinions.

3. *Poor Richard's Almanac*

   _____ a. gave advice about farming.

   _____ b. gave advice about family problems.

4. Franklin believed that religious freedom was

   _____ a. not possible.

   _____ b. important.

5. Franklin

   _____ a. was always against slavery.

   _____ b. changed his mind about slavery.

6. Franklin asked France to

   _____ a. end taxes.

   _____ b. help the United States.

7. The U.S. Constitution

   _____ a. created a new kind of government.

   _____ b. ended the American Revolution.

*"There can be . . .
no such thing
as public liberty
without freedom
of speech."*

—*Benjamin Franklin*[2]

Sequence

Work with a partner. Number the events in the correct order.

_____ Franklin opens his own print shop.

_____ Franklin helps write the U.S. Constitution.

_____ Franklin moves to Philadelphia.

_____ Franklin helps write the Treaty of Paris.

_____ Franklin begins publishing *Poor Richard's Almanac.*

Vocabulary

Look at these words from the reading. Put a check next to words that you know. Underline words that you don't know yet. Find the words in the reading. Try to guess their meanings.

bifocal	conservative	places of worship	sense of humor
chests	document	quarreled	tolerant

Use the words to fill in the blanks in the sentences.

1. Franklin thought that life in Boston was _____ and old-fashioned.

2. Franklin had a good _____ and liked jokes.

3. Franklin often argued, or _____, with his brother James.

4. Eyeglasses with _____ lenses can help people see both close up and far away.

5. In a _____ society, people with different beliefs can worship freely.

6. Churches, mosques, synagogues, and temples are _____.

7. Tea was shipped in _____, or wooden boxes, in the 1700s.

8. The Treaty of Paris was the _____ that ended the American Revolution.

Reading a Time Line

A time line shows dates and events in order on a line.

Benjamin Franklin's Life

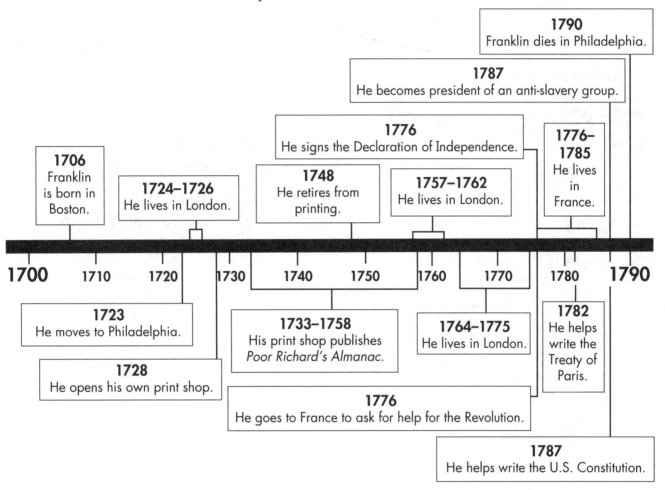

Fill in the blanks. Use information from the time line.

1. Franklin opened his own print shop at age _____.

2. Franklin's shop published *Poor Richard's Almanac* for _____ years.

3. In _____, Franklin signed the Declaration of Independence.

4. Franklin lived in France for _____ years.

5. Franklin became president of an anti-slavery society _____ years

   before he died.

John Adams said about Franklin, "He was a great genius."[4]

Do you agree? Why or why not?

Connecting Today and Yesterday

1. Franklin didn't try to hide his mistakes. For example, he publicly changed his mind about slavery. Do politicians usually try to hide their mistakes today? Give examples.

2. Franklin believed in freedom for all religions. Do you think that all religions have freedom in the United States today?

Group Activities

1. Find a copy of *Poor Richard's Almanac.* Read some of the advice with your group. Is the advice still useful today?

2. Franklin asked the British government to end the tax on tea. In your group, list three things you want the U.S. government to do today. Why are these things important?

Class Discussion

1. Franklin is called "the most human . . . of the Founding Fathers."[3] Does that name fit him? Why or why not?

2. What freedoms were most important to Franklin? Explain.

3. Franklin did many different things in his life. Which was most important for the United States? Explain your opinion.

Reflections

1. What was the most interesting thing that you read in this lesson?

2. How can you learn more about Benjamin Franklin or life during the American Revolution?

Sacagawea

"She could read rivers."

—Erica Funkhouser, about Sacagawea[1]

Pre-Reading Questions

1. Read the words under the title. What do you think that they mean?

2. Imagine someone has to travel in the wilderness. What skills are important? Why?

Reading Preview

Sacagawea was a brave Native American woman. In 1805, she started on a long journey with Lewis and Clark.

Sacagawea

Sacagawea was a Native American woman. When she was still a teenager, she was part of one of the great adventures in U.S. history. She traveled across North America with Lewis and Clark. And she helped to make their journey a success.

Sacagawea came from the Shoshone tribe in eastern Idaho. Around 1800, when she was about 12 years old, the enemy Hidatsa tribe captured her. They sold her to the Mandan tribe near Bismarck, North Dakota. Later, the Mandans sold her to Toussaint Charbonneau, a Canadian fur trader. She became one of his wives.

In November 1804, Charbonneau and his wives were living near Fort Mandan. A group of men arrived in the area. The leaders were Meriwether Lewis and William Clark. They were exploring the land between the Missouri River and the Pacific Ocean. The group stayed in Fort Mandan for the winter.

In April 1805, Lewis and Clark were ready to continue. But they knew that they would meet many different Native American tribes. They needed someone to translate. So they hired Charbonneau. They asked Sacagawea to go on the journey too. Charbonneau spoke French and Hidatsa. Sacagawea spoke Hidatsa and her native Shoshone.

Charbonneau and Sacagawea joined the group. At the time, Sacagawea had a two-month-old baby. His name was Jean Baptiste. She carried him on her back. Clark became fond of the baby. He gave him the nickname "Pomp."

Sacagawea was the only woman on the journey. She helped Lewis and Clark in many ways. She translated when they met Native Americans. She knew how to find edible plants. She was pleasant and helpful.

When the group met Native Americans, the Native Americans were worried at first. They thought these white men could be enemies. But then they saw Sacagawea and her child. They felt safe. They knew that only a peaceful group would have a woman and baby with them. Sacagawea "was a sign of peace."[2]

In May 1805, Sacagawea saved Lewis and Clark from

disaster. The group was traveling by river. A strong wind nearly knocked over one of their boats. Many supplies fell into the water. Papers, medicine, mapping supplies, and other important things were floating away. Sacagawea was in the boat. She stayed calm and quickly pulled papers and equipment from the water. Lewis later wrote that she was as brave as anyone who was in the boat.

When the group reached the Shoshone lands, Sacagawea got an amazing surprise. They met the Shoshone leader, Cameahwait. Sacagawea immediately recognized him: he was her brother! They hadn't seen each other in five years. Sacagawea spoke to her brother, and he gave the group the horses that they needed. Sacagawea could have stayed with her brother and her Shoshone people. But she chose to stay with Lewis and Clark.

The group continued west. On November 7, 1805, they finally saw the Pacific Ocean. They spent the winter on the Pacific coast at Fort Clatsop, Oregon. In the spring, they started traveling back east again.

When they reached Fort Mandan, Sacagawea, Pomp, and Charbonneau left the group. The U.S. government paid Charbonneau around $500. That was a lot of money at the time. Later, they gave him 320 acres of land, too. Sacagawea did not receive anything.

People don't know much about Sacagawea's later life. Most historians think that she had a baby girl in 1812 and died soon after that. She was about 25 years old.

After Sacagawea died, Charbonneau left Pomp with William Clark. Clark provided for the boy. He sent Pomp to school in St. Louis. He also paid for the boy's housing, food, and clothes. There is little information about Sacagawea's daughter. She may have died young.

In 1998, the U.S. government was planning a new gold-colored dollar coin. The U.S. Mint decided to put Sacagawea on the coin. But there was a problem. There are no pictures of her. No one knows what she looked like.

Finally, artist Glenna Goodacre used a contemporary

"Sacagawea [was] a courageous, determined, and admirable Indian woman."[3]

Shoshone woman as a model. The coin shows Sacagawea carrying her baby on her back.

The United States began using the Sacagawea dollar in January 2000. It is a way for people to honor and remember a remarkable young woman.

Comprehension

Complete the sentences. Use information from the reading.

1. When Sacagawea was about 12 years old, _____

   _____.

2. Sacagawea and Charbonneau joined Lewis and Clark because _____

   _____

   _____.

3. When Lewis and Clark arrived in Shoshone lands, _____

   _____.

4. To help Lewis and Clark, Sacagawea _____

   _____.

5. When other Native Americans saw Sacagawea and her baby, _____

   _____

   _____.

6. After Sacagawea died, Clark _____

   _____.

7. The gold-colored dollar uses a picture of a contemporary woman because _____

   _____

   _____.

Fact or Opinion

Work with a partner. Decide if each sentence is a fact or an opinion. Then write *F* for *fact* or *O* for *opinion* in front of each sentence.

_____ 1. Lewis and Clark needed Sacagawea.

_____ 2. Sacagawea had many skills that helped Lewis and Clark.

_____ 3. Sacagawea was brave.

_____ 4. Clark helped Sacagawea's family.

Vocabulary

Look at these words from the reading. Put a check next to words that you know. Underline words that you don't know yet. Find the words in the reading. Try to guess their meanings.

| contemporary | edible | nickname | trader |
| disaster | honor | provide for | translate |

Match each word with its definition.

_____ 1. trader   a. to remember with respect

_____ 2. translate   b. modern

_____ 3. nickname   c. to put into another language

_____ 4. edible   d. to take care of

_____ 5. disaster   e. a friendly name, often short

_____ 6. provide for   f. OK to eat

_____ 7. contemporary   g. businessman

_____ 8. honor   h. failure; great loss

Reading a Map

Physical maps show features of the land and water. **Political maps** show borders between countries, states, or other political regions. **Historical maps** show features from the past. Some maps, like this one, combine all three types. It shows physical features and contemporary political regions in North America. It also shows the route of Sacagawea's journey with Lewis and Clark.

Sacagawea's Journey with Lewis and Clark

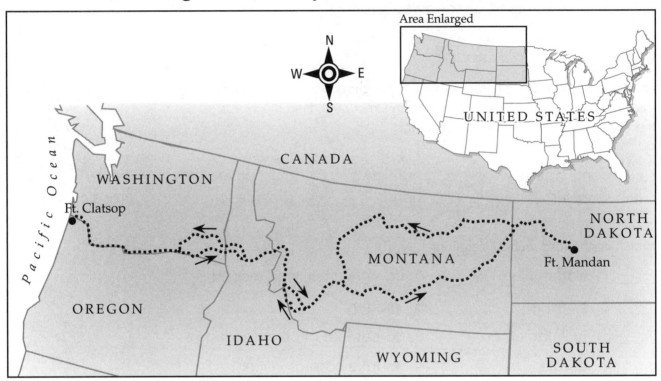

Answer the questions. Use information from the map.

1. How many states did Sacagawea travel through? _____

2. List the names of the states. _____

   _____

3. What was the name of the fort where she began and ended her trip? _____

   _____

4. What state is Fort Clatsop in? _____

5. Why would Lewis and Clark stop there? _____

   _____

Connecting Today and Yesterday

1. The name *Sacagawea* means "Bird Woman" in the Hidatsa language. Does your name have a special meaning? If yes, what is it?

2. An enemy tribe kidnapped Sacagawea. Is kidnapping a problem today?

Group Activities

1. With your group, make a list of three ways Sacagawea helped Lewis and Clark. Discuss why each one was important.

2. Find a Sacagawea dollar or a picture of one. Look at it with your group. What do you think Sacagawea looked like?

Class Discussion

1. Why do you think that Sacagawea stayed with Lewis and Clark and didn't stay with her brother?

2. What was Sacagawea's life like before she met Lewis and Clark? How did the journey change her life? Explain your opinion.

3. What was Sacagawea's biggest problem on the journey? Explain your opinion.

Reflections

1. What was the most interesting thing that you read in this lesson?

2. Can you use anything from Sacagawea's story in your own life? Explain.

There are more parks, statues, and songs for Sacagawea than for any other woman in U.S. history.

Why? Explain your opinion.

Abraham Lincoln

"A house divided against itself cannot stand."

—Abraham Lincoln[1]

Pre-Reading Questions

1. Read the words under the title. What do you think that they mean?

2. Is it important for a country to stay united? What problems happen when large groups disagree?

Reading Preview

Abraham Lincoln is one of the most honored men in U.S. history. He helped preserve the country in the Civil War. And he helped abolish slavery.

Abraham Lincoln

Abraham Lincoln was president during the worst crisis in U.S. history. The issue of slavery divided the country. It started a bloody civil war. Lincoln helped preserve the country and end slavery.

Abraham Lincoln was born on February 12, 1809, in Hardin, Kentucky. When he was a child, his family moved to Indiana. They were farmers. Lincoln went to school for only a year. But he learned to read and always loved books.

When he grew up, Lincoln moved to New Salem, Illinois. He became the town's postmaster in 1833. In 1834, he was elected to the Illinois state government. In his spare time, he studied law. He became a lawyer in 1836.

Lincoln served in the state government until 1842. In 1846, he ran for Congress. He won and served a two-year term. Then he went back to practicing law. He became one of the best-known lawyers in Illinois.

Lincoln also stayed active in politics. He wanted to keep slavery out of new U.S. territories. He worked for that goal in state and national politics. In 1856, he joined the new Republican Party. The Republicans opposed slavery.

In 1858, Lincoln ran for the U.S. Senate. He was running against Stephen A. Douglas. Douglas supported the Kansas–Nebraska Act. Under this law, people in new territories could vote to allow slavery. Lincoln and Douglas had seven famous debates. Douglas won the race. But people around the country heard about Lincoln. In 1860, he ran for president. The other parties were divided. Lincoln won easily.

The southern states were afraid that President Lincoln would end slavery. After the election, 11 southern states seceded, or left the union. They formed a new government called the Confederacy. The Confederacy wanted U.S. troops to leave the South. Lincoln promised to protect U.S. property in the South. On April 12, 1861, southern soldiers attacked Fort Sumter in South Carolina. This attack began the Civil War.

Lincoln believed strongly in democratic government. He wanted to show the world that a democratic country could handle this crisis. He also believed that slavery was evil.

But his first goal was to keep the country united. Many northerners would fight for that, but not to end slavery. Lincoln focused on preserving the union.

But as the war dragged on, public opinion changed. More northerners wanted to end slavery. Lincoln decided that it was time to move against slavery. In January 1863, he signed the Emancipation Proclamation. This document said that the slaves in the Confederacy were free. Four slave states were still in the union. Lincoln urged them to free their slaves too.

In 1864, the North won several major battles. These battles encouraged northern voters. They re-elected Lincoln. He began his second term in March 1865. The war was nearly won. Lincoln asked the country to show mercy to the defeated South. He wanted peace between the regions.

On April 9, 1865, southern forces surrendered to General Ulysses S. Grant. The war was over. But many southerners felt humiliated. They lost property, family, and their lifestyle. So Lincoln had many enemies. On April 14, 1865, he went to a play at Ford's Theatre in Washington, D.C. John Wilkes Booth, a famous southern actor, was also there. He went to Lincoln's seat and shot him in the head. Lincoln died the next day. This was the first time a U.S. president was assassinated.

Lincoln didn't live to see the end of slavery in the United States. But he made it possible. In December 1865, the 13th Amendment to the U.S. Constitution outlawed slavery.

Lincoln is probably the most popular president in U.S. history. He helped to free the slaves. And he kept the United States one country.

Comprehension

Check the correct answer.

1. To become a lawyer, Lincoln
   _____ a. studied law by himself.
   _____ b. went to a good law school.

2. Because of the debates with Douglas,
   _____ a. people learned about Lincoln.
   _____ b. Lincoln was elected to the U.S. Senate.

3. When Lincoln became president,
   _____ a. he ended slavery.
   _____ b. 11 states seceded.

4. The attack on Fort Sumter
   _____ a. ended the Civil War.
   _____ b. began the Civil War.

5. When the Civil War started, Lincoln's first goal was
   _____ a. ending slavery.
   _____ b. keeping the country united.

6. The Emancipation Proclamation
   _____ a. freed the slaves in the Confederacy.
   _____ b. freed the slaves in the United States.

7. Lincoln was assassinated
   _____ a. at the end of his first term.
   _____ b. at the beginning of his second term.

The battle of Antietam, Maryland, lasted three days—September 16–18, 1862. The second day of battle was the bloodiest single day of the Civil War. There were more than 23,000 casualties, North and South, on September 17, 1862.[2]

Sequence

Work with a partner. Number the events in the correct order.

_____ The Civil War begins.

_____ Lincoln becomes a lawyer.

_____ The 13th Amendment is passed.

_____ Lincoln is assassinated.

_____ Lincoln debates Douglas.

Vocabulary

Look at these words from the reading. Put a check next to words that you know. Underline words that you don't know yet. Find the words in the reading. Try to guess their meanings.

assassinated	debates	humiliated	surrendered
crisis	democratic	preserve	territories

Use the words to fill in the blanks in the sentences.

1. The Civil War was the worst _____ in U.S. history.

2. During the war, Lincoln's first goal was to _____ the country.

3. U.S. _____ were part of the country, but they weren't states.

4. In their famous _____, Lincoln and Douglas spoke about the Kansas–Nebraska Act.

5. Lincoln believed in a _____ form of government.

6. The Civil War ended when southern forces _____ to General Grant.

7. Many southerners felt _____ because they lost so much in the war.

8. John Wilkes Booth _____ Lincoln.

Reading a Chart

A chart is a useful way to organize facts.

The North and South in the Civil War[3]

	North	South
Total population	26,200,000	8,100,000
Number of soldiers	2,800,000	1,000,000
Number killed in combat	359,528	198,524
Number wounded	275,175	137,000
Number who died of other causes (disease, prison, etc.)	249,458	124,000
Financial cost (in 1990 dollars)	$27.3 billion	$17.1 billion

Answer the questions. Use information from the chart.

1. Which army had more men? _____

2. Why was this army larger? _____

3. Which army had more men killed? _____

4. Why? _____

5. What was the total number of soldiers wounded? _____

6. Do you think that this number is large?_____

   _____

7. What was the total financial cost of the Civil War? _____

8. Who do you think paid for the war? _____

   _____

9. Does any of this information surprise you? _____

   _____

More than 5,000 books have been written about Abraham Lincoln.

Why? Explain your opinion.

Connecting Today and Yesterday

1. The issue of slavery divided the United States in the 1800s. Do any important issues divide the United States today? If yes, what are they?

2. Booth opposed Lincoln's policies, so he assassinated Lincoln. Do people still assassinate leaders? If yes, why? Do they oppose the person? The person's policies? Are there other reasons?

Group Activity

Three other U.S. presidents have been assassinated. Research these questions. Then discuss the answers in your group.

1. Which other presidents were assassinated?

2. When were they assassinated?

3. Why were they assassinated?

4. Who killed them?

5. What happened to John Wilkes Booth? What happened to the people who killed the other presidents?

Class Discussion

1. Lincoln hated slavery. But ending slavery was not his first goal. Do you think that was a good policy? Why or why not?

2. Both the North and the South thought that the war would be quick. Each side thought that it would win. Does this kind of attitude about war still exist today? Explain.

3. Lincoln had very little formal education. He went to school for only a year. But he led the United States through its worst crisis. How was he able to do that? Explain your opinion.

Reflections

1. What was the most interesting thing that you read in this lesson?

2. How can you learn more about Abraham Lincoln or the U.S. Civil War?

Harriet Tubman

"I was free; but dere was no one to welcome me to de land of freedom. I was a stranger in a strange land."

—Harriet Tubman[1]

Pre-Reading Questions

1. Read the words under the title. What do you think that they mean? Why did Tubman feel like a stranger in a strange land?

2. The writer wrote "dere" for *there* and "de" for *the* to show how Tubman spoke. Is this a good idea? Is it confusing? Explain your opinion.

Reading Preview

Harriet Tubman was a slave who escaped. She led more than 300 slaves to freedom on the Underground Railroad. She also worked for the northern army in the Civil War.

Harriet Tubman

Before the United States abolished slavery, many slaves tried to escape to freedom. They often traveled north on the Underground Railroad. The most famous conductor on the Railroad was Harriet Tubman.

Harriet Tubman was born a slave in Dorchester County, Maryland, around 1820. By the time she was 12, she was working in the cotton fields. The work was exhausting and difficult.

Early in her life, Tubman showed strong compassion for other people. When she was about 12 years old, the slave boss told her to help tie up another slave. Tubman refused. The slave boss hit her in the head with a brick. It was nearly fatal. It took her a long time to recover. She always had an ugly scar. And for the rest of her life, she had sudden periods of unconsciousness.

In 1849, Tubman was afraid that her owner was going to sell her to someone in Georgia. She ran away. She went to the home of a friendly white neighbor. The neighbor told Tubman how to find other helpful people and safe places. After a dangerous trip, Tubman arrived in Pennsylvania, a free state.

Soon Tubman got a job cooking and washing dishes in a hotel kitchen. She also met William Still, a successful black merchant in Philadelphia. He was an organizer of the Underground Railroad.

The Underground Railroad was a secret network of roads, rivers, and safe houses. Escaping slaves could hide and rest in the safe houses. People would give them food, clothes, and travel directions.

Traveling on this route was dangerous. A slave who was caught could be severely punished. Some people traveled alone or with other escaping slaves. And some people followed a "conductor." Conductors led slaves on the escape route.

Tubman learned about this secret network from Still. She wanted to help other slaves get to freedom. Her first chance to be a conductor came soon. In 1851, she helped her sister and her sister's children escape from Baltimore to Philadelphia.

Over the next 16 years, Tubman made 18 more trips as a conductor on the Underground Railroad. She protected her "passengers" fiercely. She carried a gun, and she threatened to shoot anyone who wanted to turn back.

Tubman was never caught, and she rescued about 300 people from slavery. Some of those people were members of her family, including her parents.

In 1863, during the Civil War, the northern army needed information about the South. The army asked Tubman to organize a team of black spies. These people would go south to gather information. Tubman herself went south on these missions. No one suspected her. They didn't think that a black woman could be a spy. She also convinced many former slaves to join the northern army to fight against slavery.

Tubman worked for the military for three years. She never got a salary. So she had to make money to support herself and her work. She sold baked goods, chickens, and root beer.

After the Civil War, Tubman went to live in Auburn, New York. Some of her family already lived there. In Auburn, she raised money for schools for freed slaves. She also worked for women's rights. In 1869, Sarah H. Bradford, an Auburn schoolteacher, wrote the story of Tubman's life. At first, it was called *Scenes in the Life of Harriet Tubman.* It was later expanded and called *Harriet, the Moses of Her People.*

In 1908, Tubman set up a home in Auburn for old and poor people. She moved into the home herself for her last two years. She died on March 10, 1913. She was about 93 years old.

Tubman was buried in Auburn with military honors. The next year, the people of Auburn put up a bronze plaque for her in the county courthouse. They also declared a holiday in her honor.

Between 30,000 and 100,000 slaves used the Underground Railroad trying to reach freedom.[2]

During World War II, a U.S. ship was named *Harriet Tubman*. The U.S. Post Office issued Harriet Tubman stamps in 1978 and in 1995. Harriet Tubman is remembered as a true American hero.

Comprehension

Complete the sentences. Use information from the reading.

1. Tubman was badly hurt when _____

   _____.

2. When Tubman got to Pennsylvania, she _____

   _____.

3. The Underground Railroad was _____

   _____.

4. The northern army asked Tubman to _____

   _____.

5. Tubman earned money for her work by _____

   _____.

6. After the Civil War, Tubman moved to Auburn, New York, because _____

   _____

   _____.

7. In 1908, Tubman set up _____

   _____.

Fact or Opinion

Work with a partner. Decide if each sentence is a fact or an opinion. Then write *F* for *fact* or *O* for *opinion* in front of each sentence.

_____ 1. A teacher wrote a book about Tubman's life.

_____ 2. The people who worked on the Underground Railroad were heroes.

_____ 3. Tubman didn't get a military salary.

_____ 4. Tubman started a home for poor and old people.

_____ 5. A U.S. ship was named for Harriet Tubman.

Vocabulary

Look at these words from the reading. Put a check next to words that you know. Underline words that you don't know yet. Find the words in the reading. Try to guess their meanings.

| compassion | fatal | military honors | plaque |
| exhausting | merchant | network | unconsciousness |

Match each word with its definition.

_____ 1. exhausting   a. special ceremonies at a solidier's funeral

_____ 2. compassion   b. causing death

_____ 3. fatal   c. a lack of awareness, like sleep

_____ 4. unconsciousness   d. wearing someone out completely

_____ 5. merchant   e. a feeling for the suffering of others

_____ 6. network   f. an engraved slab, usually made of metal or stone

_____ 7. military honors   g. someone who buys and sells goods

_____ 8. plaque   h. a group of things that are connected in complicated ways

Reading a Chart

A chart is a useful way to organize facts. This chart has information about quilt patterns. Some writers say that quilts had hidden messages about the Underground Railroad.[3] A quilt hung outside might tell a slave that it was safe to leave or what route to follow.

Hidden Meanings in Quilts?

Pattern	Name of pattern	Possible hidden meaning
	Monkey Wrench	Get your tools, such as a compass and a knife. Get ready to leave.
	Bear Paw	Follow bear tracks (probably through the Appalachian Mountains).
	Flying Geese	Travel like the geese. Go north. Rest near water.
	Drunkard's Path	Take a crooked path to avoid slave catchers.

Answer the questions. Use information from the chart.

1. What would a Monkey Wrench quilt tell someone to do? _____

_____

2. How would you tell someone to follow birds? _____

3. What animal's trail should people follow through the mountains? _____

4. Why would people who were escaping follow a "drunkard's path"? _____

_____

5. Many people say that this is a nice story, but not true.

   Do you think that people could use quilts this way? Why or why not? _____

_____

Connecting Today and Yesterday

1. Tubman worked for the U.S. military. Today, many women join the military. Do you think that women should be in the military? Should they do the same jobs as men do?

2. During the Civil War, Tubman gathered information about the South. She had to go south to do this. Today, the U.S. government uses technology to gather information. Do we need people to gather information too? Explain your opinion.

Group Activity

Find out more about the Underground Railroad. Then discuss these questions in your group.

1. Where did it go?

2. How many people did it help?

3. When did most escaping slaves travel?

4. Did any slaves escape and not use the Underground Railroad?

Class Discussion

1. Why would Tubman risk her life to rescue slaves?

2. The 1978 Harriet Tubman postage stamp was the first in a series called "Black Heritage USA." Why did the Post Office choose Tubman for the first stamp?

3. Why did Bradford call Tubman's biography *Harriet, the Moses of Her People*? Who was Moses? How were Moses and Tubman alike?

Reflections

1. What was the most interesting thing that you read in this lesson?

2. Can you use anything from Harriet Tubman's story in your own life? Explain.

Tubman said, "I never ran my train off the track, and I never lost a passenger."[4]

What did she mean?

Mark Twain

"Whatever you have lived, you can write; . . . but what you have not lived you cannot write."

—Mark Twain[1]

HUCKLEBERRY FINN.

Pre-Reading Questions

1. Read the words under the title. What do you think that they mean?

2. Do you think that a writer must live something to write about it? Explain your opinion.

Reading Preview

Mark Twain used humor to talk about difficult issues. He was one of the most important writers and public speakers in U.S. history.

Mark Twain

In the 1800s, life was an adventure for a kid in Hannibal, Missouri. The village was on the Mississippi River. Children loved to watch the steamboats. There were caves and woods to explore. Sometimes the circus came to town. Mark Twain spent his childhood there.

Mark Twain's real name was Samuel Clemens. He was born in Missouri in 1835. In 1839, his family moved to Hannibal. When he was 12 years old, his father died. Twain quit school and got a job at the local newspaper. The newspaper trained him as a printer. Four years later, he went to work in his brother Orion's print shop. Sometimes he was an editor, and sometimes he wrote. He liked to write humorous, or funny, articles.

In 1857, Twain decided to become a steamboat pilot on the Mississippi River. He got his pilot's license in 1859. But in 1861, the Civil War stopped steamboat traffic on the river. So he moved to Nevada.

Twain became a reporter for a newspaper in Nevada. He wrote daily stories about events there. He wrote in a conversational style that was easy to understand. Sometimes he mixed humorous fiction with the real news. He used made-up information to make a story better or funnier.

In 1863, he began to sign his stories "Mark Twain." Steamboat pilots used the term *mark twain*. It meant "12 feet deep." That was the place where water became too shallow and dangerous for the boats.

Twain moved on to California. He worked for newspapers there. In 1865, he published his first popular story. It was about a frog-jumping contest.

In 1866, a newspaper sent Twain to Hawaii. When he returned, he started a successful public-speaking tour. At the time, public speakers were popular entertainment. Twain's topics included politics, everyday life, and human nature, or the way people act. He was not afraid to joke about famous people and to laugh at himself.

In 1870, Twain married Olivia Langdon. They moved to Hartford, Connecticut. While they lived there, Twain wrote his two most famous novels: *The Adventures of Tom Sawyer* and *The Adventures of Huckleberry Finn.*

The Adventures of Tom Sawyer was published in 1876. It was about the fun and adventures of childhood. Twain used his own memories of his childhood in Hannibal. The book was popular. *The Adventures of Huckleberry Finn* was published in 1885. It included humor too, but it also explored the morality of slavery. Many people believe that it was Twain's greatest work.

The book told the story of Tom Sawyer's friend, Huckleberry Finn. Huck runs away to an island to escape his violent father. There he becomes friends with Jim, a runaway slave. He decides not to report Jim to the police. Instead, he travels with Jim north to freedom.

Not everyone liked *Huckleberry Finn.* The story is told from Huck's viewpoint. Twain wrote informally, in the way that a boy like Huck would speak. This was the first time in American literature that an author used such informal language. Some readers objected to the bad grammar and vulgar words. Others objected because the hero, Huck Finn, broke the law. The public library in Concord, Massachusetts, banned the book in 1885.

Today, some people still object to the book. They don't like the way it shows black people and the racial language. But others say that it teaches about human equality and the dangers of prejudice. It is used in many schools.

In the 1880s and 1890s, Twain lost money in investments. In 1895, he couldn't pay his bills. He traveled around the world on a public-speaking tour. He earned enough money to solve his financial problems. But he had repeated personal tragedies. Between 1896 and 1909, his wife and two of his daughters died. He kept writing, but his later works were sadder and more pessimistic.

Mark Twain created a truly American writing style. It showed the way American people really talked. When he died in 1910, newspapers said that the whole world was mourning.[2]

Comprehension

Check the correct answer.

1. Twain was known for writing

    _____ a. humorous stories.

    _____ b. serious news stories.

2. Twain's job as a steamboat pilot ended when

    _____ a. Twain became a soldier in the Civil War.

    _____ b. the Civil War stopped steamboat traffic.

3. Twain wrote

    _____ a. in a conversational style.

    _____ b. in a formal style.

4. *The Adventures of Tom Sawyer* was about

    _____ a. the fun of childhood.

    _____ b. the morality of slavery.

5. In *The Adventures of Huckleberry Finn,* Huck

    _____ a. traveled with Jim to freedom.

    _____ b. reported Jim to the law.

6. In his later years, Twain

    _____ a. had many troubles.

    _____ b. led a peaceful life.

7. In his lifetime, Twain

    _____ a. lived in Hannibal, Missouri, most of the time.

    _____ b. traveled widely.

Sequence

Work with a partner. Number the events in the correct order.

_____ Clemens starts using the name *Mark Twain.*

_____ Twain marries Olivia Langdon.

_____ Twain is bankrupt.

_____ Twain writes *Huckleberry Finn.*

_____ Twain works as a steamboat pilot.

_____ Twain publishes a story about a frog-jumping contest.

Vocabulary

Look at these words from the reading. Put a check next to words that you know. Underline words that you don't know yet. Find the words in the reading. Try to guess their meanings.

conversational	humorous	mourned	pilot
human nature	morality	pessimistic	vulgar

Use the words to fill in the blanks in the sentences.

1. Many of Twain's stories were _____, or funny.

2. Twain became a _____ for steamboats on the Mississippi River.

3. Twain's _____ writing style sounded like people talking.

4. The way that people naturally behave is called _____.

5. The word _____ means ideas about right or wrong.

6. Some of the language in *Huckleberry Finn* was _____, or rude.

7. Twain's writing was more gloomy and _____ in his later life.

8. The world _____ when Twain died.

Reading a Time Line

A time line shows dates and events in order on a line.

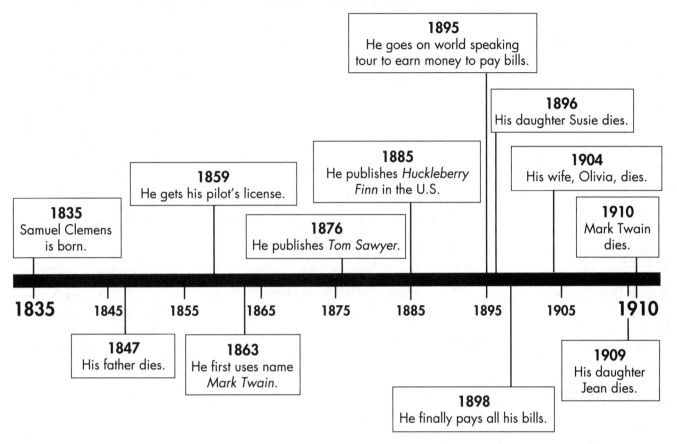

Mark Twain's Life

1895
He goes on world speaking tour to earn money to pay bills.

1896
His daughter Susie dies.

1885
He publishes *Huckleberry Finn* in the U.S.

1904
His wife, Olivia, dies.

1859
He gets his pilot's license.

1910
Mark Twain dies.

1835
Samuel Clemens is born.

1876
He publishes *Tom Sawyer.*

1835 1845 1855 1865 1875 1885 1895 1905 1910

1847
His father dies.

1863
He first uses name *Mark Twain.*

1909
His daughter Jean dies.

1898
He finally pays all his bills.

Fill in the blanks. Use information from the time line.

1. Twain was _____ years old when he got his pilot's license.

2. Samuel Clemens began using the name *Mark Twain* when he was

    _____ years old.

3. Twain published *Huckleberry Finn* in the United States _____

    years after he published *Tom Sawyer.*

4. Twain went on a speaking tour in 1895 because _____

    _____.

5. After his wife died, Twain lived for_____ more years.

6. Twain was _____ years old when he died.

Twain read a book about the French Revolution by Thomas Carlyle. In it, Carlyle wrote, "A lie cannot live." Twain said, "It shows that he did not know how to tell them."[5]

What did he mean by that?

Connecting Today and Yesterday

1. Twain's books are still popular today. What qualities make a book popular for many years?

2. Soon after *Huckleberry Finn* was published, a library banned it. Today, some schools don't teach it. Do you think that libraries should ban a book? Do you think that schools should refuse to teach a book? Why or why not?

Group Activities

1. Mark Twain was a master storyteller. He told tall tales. He took the truth and made it bigger and better. For example, in a story about fishing, the fish would be bigger each time he told the story. Do you know any tall tales? If so, share them with your group.

2. Watch the movie *The Adventures of Tom Sawyer* or *The Adventures of Huckleberry Finn* with your group. Discuss what you like and don't like. Did anything surprise you?

3. Bring in a book with humorous quotations by Mark Twain. Read some to your group. Discuss their meaning.

Class Discussion

1. Why would Clemens use the name *Mark Twain*? Remember that it means a place where water becomes too shallow and dangerous.

2. Mark Twain wrote, "Good friends, good books and a sleepy conscience: this is the ideal life."[4] What do you think that he meant? Do you agree? Why or why not?

3. Twain wrote *Huckleberry Finn* in the same informal way that people talked. He showed people's real ideas and behavior, good and bad. Do you think that it is a good idea to write this way? Why or why not?

Reflections

1. What was the most interesting thing that you read in this lesson?

2. How can you learn more about Mark Twain or his work?

Theodore Roosevelt

> *"Speak softly
> and carry a big stick."*
>
> —*Theodore Roosevelt*[1]

Pre-Reading Questions

1. Read the words under the title. What do you think that they mean?

2. In politics, how does someone "speak softly and carry a big stick"? Is it a good idea? Is it dangerous? Explain your opinion.

Reading Preview

Theodore Roosevelt was a very popular U.S. president. He acted strongly in foreign policy. He helped preserve millions of acres of natural land.

Theodore Roosevelt

The years 1890 to 1913 were called The Progressive Era. The United States was optimistic and moving forward. But it also had problems. When President William McKinley was killed in 1901, Theodore Roosevelt became president. "Teddy" Roosevelt kept the country moving forward.

Roosevelt was born in 1858. He was sickly and had poor eyesight. But he had a strong mind. And he was an active child. He exercised regularly and made his body strong too.

Roosevelt loved nature. He kept a nature museum at home. He collected specimens of every animal and insect he could find. He even paid friends to find new ones. When he attended Harvard University, he studied natural history.

After college, Roosevelt studied law. But law bored him. He liked politics instead. He ran for the New York State Assembly in 1881 and won. He was 23 years old. He was re-elected in 1882 and 1883.

Then, in 1884, his wife and his mother died on the same day. Roosevelt left politics and mourned. He became a rancher in the Dakota Territory. He worked up to 16 hours a day. He also wrote history books. In 1886, he remarried. In time, he and his second wife, Edith, had five children. They also raised his daughter from his first marriage.

Also in 1886, Roosevelt returned to politics. He ran for mayor of New York City, but lost. In 1888, he became a member of the Civil Service Commission. And in 1895, he became police commissioner of New York City. In that job, he made many reforms. In 1896, President William McKinley made Roosevelt assistant secretary of the Navy. Roosevelt came to see that sea power was important in the modern world.

In 1898, Cuban rebels were fighting for freedom from Spain. The United States entered the war on the rebels' side. Roosevelt quit his job. He gathered a volunteer group to fight in Cuba. They were called The Rough Riders. On July 1, Roosevelt led his men in a charge. They attacked Spanish troops on San Juan Hill. The battle made them famous. Roosevelt became a national hero.

After the war, Roosevelt became governor of New York. In 1900, President McKinley was running for a second term. He chose Roosevelt to run for vice president.

McKinley was re-elected. But he was killed in September 1901, just six months after he started his second term. Roosevelt became president. He was 42 years old, the youngest president in U.S. history.

As president, Roosevelt was still a reformer. He worked to limit the power of big companies. He supported striking mine workers. Early in his term, he invited Booker T. Washington to eat at the White House. Washington was a well-known black leader and educator. He had been born a slave. Many whites were shocked. They did not think that blacks and whites should mix.

Roosevelt also worked to conserve open land. In 1905, he signed the law that created the U.S. Forest Service. It protected about 150 million acres of forest. He created 51 refuges for birds and 4 game preserves for animals. Hunting was not allowed in those places.

Roosevelt was also a leader in foreign policy. He expanded and modernized the U.S. Navy. He wanted Navy ships to move more quickly between the Atlantic and Pacific Oceans. So he wanted to build a canal across Panama. He started talks with Colombia. At the time, Panama was part of Colombia. The talks reached agreement, but Colombia's senate voted against it. So Roosevelt supported rebels in Panama. He sent 10 warships to the coast of Panama. Panama became independent. And it agreed to let the United States build the canal.

In his second term, Roosevelt mediated the end of a war between Russia and Japan. The next year, he received the Nobel Peace Prize. He was the first American to win this prize.

After his second term ended in 1908, Roosevelt traveled. In 1912, he ran for president again. He lost the election and retired from active politics. But he still spoke out on political issues.

Roosevelt went bear hunting in 1902, but he didn't find any bears. Finally, his guides cornered a bear for him. But the bear was hurt, and Roosevelt refused to shoot it. This story became famous. One shopkeeper sold some toy bears that he called "Teddy's bears." Soon, many toy companies were making stuffed bears called "teddy bears."

In 1914, Roosevelt took a trip to Africa. He got a tropical illness there. He was never completely well again. He died on January 6, 1919.

Comprehension

Complete the sentences. Use information from the reading.

1. The years 1890–1916 were called the Progressive Era because _____

   _____

   _____.

2. As a child, Roosevelt _____

   _____.

3. When Cuba was fighting for independence, Roosevelt _____

   _____.

4. Some whites were upset when Booker T. Washington ate with Roosevelt

   because _____

   _____.

5. Roosevelt sent U.S. warships to Panama because _____

   _____.

6. After it was created, the U.S. Forest Service _____

   _____.

7. Roosevelt received the Nobel Peace Prize because he _____

   _____.

Fact or Opinion

Work with a partner. Decide if each sentence is a fact or an opinion. Then write *F* for *fact* or *O* for *opinion* in front of each sentence.

_____ 1. Roosevelt left politics after his wife and mother died.

_____ 2. It was sad that Roosevelt's wife and mother died on the same day.

_____ 3. Roosevelt wanted a strong military and a strong foreign policy.

_____ 4. Getting the Panama Canal was more important than how Roosevelt got it.

Vocabulary

Look at these words from the reading. Put a check next to words that you know. Underline words that you don't know yet. Find the words in the reading. Try to guess their meanings.

charge	game preserve	optimistic	specimen
conserve	mediate	refuge	tropical

Match each word with its definition.

_____ 1. optimistic   a. to help others solve problems by talking

_____ 2. specimen   b. strong, rushing attack

_____ 3. charge   c. sample

_____ 4. conserve   d. cheerful; expecting good things to happen

_____ 5. refuge   e. place where hunting is not allowed

_____ 6. game preserve   f. safe place

_____ 7. mediate   g. from a very hot, humid climate

_____ 8. tropical   h. to protect

Reading a Time Line

A time line shows dates and events in order on a line.

Conserving Nature: Theodore Roosevelt

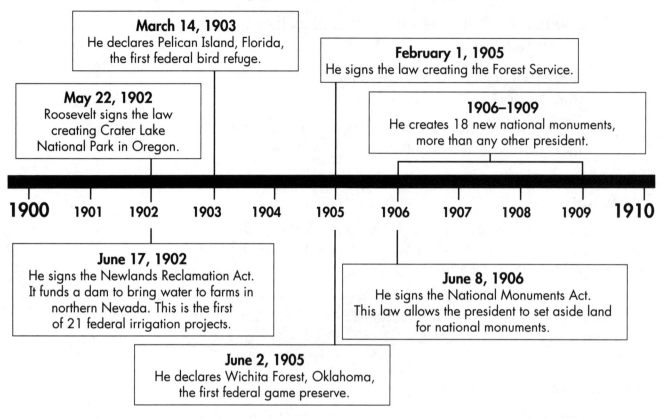

March 14, 1903
He declares Pelican Island, Florida, the first federal bird refuge.

February 1, 1905
He signs the law creating the Forest Service.

May 22, 1902
Roosevelt signs the law creating Crater Lake National Park in Oregon.

1906–1909
He creates 18 new national monuments, more than any other president.

1900   1901   1902   1903   1904   1905   1906   1907   1908   1909   1910

June 17, 1902
He signs the Newlands Reclamation Act. It funds a dam to bring water to farms in northern Nevada. This is the first of 21 federal irrigation projects.

June 8, 1906
He signs the National Monuments Act. This law allows the president to set aside land for national monuments.

June 2, 1905
He declares Wichita Forest, Oklahoma, the first federal game preserve.

Answer the questions. Use information from the time line.

1. When did Roosevelt declare the first federal bird refuge? _____

2. Which act allows presidents to create national monuments? _____

   _____

3. Which national park was in Oregon? _____

4. What year was the park created? _____

5. Which of Roosevelt's actions was most important for the future?

   Explain your opinion. _____

   _____

Connecting Today and Yesterday

1. The United States sent warships to help Panama become independent. How does the United States use the military in foreign policy today?

2. Roosevelt used photographs from Cuba to make himself look brave and adventurous. Do pictures in newspapers and on TV affect the images of politicians today? Explain.

Group Activity

Research the history of the Panama Canal. Bring information and pictures to share with your group. Then discuss these questions.

1. When France tried to build the canal, what problems did it have? Why did it give up?

2. Why was malaria important in the history of the canal?

3. How long did it take the United States to build the canal? When did the canal open?

4. Who owns the Panama Canal today?

5. Is the Panama Canal still important for the United States? Explain.

Class Discussion

1. Roosevelt believed that it was a good idea to "speak softly and carry a big stick." How did he use this idea in building the Panama Canal?

2. Conserving open land was important to Roosevelt. Do you think that conserving open land is still important today? Why or why not?

Reflections

1. What was the most interesting thing that you read in this lesson?

2. Can you use anything from Theodore Roosevelt's story in your own life? Explain.

Roosevelt said, "I took Panama and let Congress debate that while I went ahead and built the canal."[2]

What did he mean?

Emma Lazarus

"I lift my lamp beside the golden door!"
(words on the Statue of Liberty)

—*Emma Lazarus*[1]

Pre-Reading Questions

1. Read the words under the title. What do you think that they mean?

2. What do you know about the Statue of Liberty?

Reading Preview

Emma Lazarus was a famous Jewish writer. One of her poems is on the Statue of Liberty.

Emma Lazarus

Emma Lazarus came from one of America's first Jewish families. Her father's family arrived in America in the 1600s. They were from Spain and Portugal. She was proud of her ancestors.

Lazarus was born on July 22, 1849, in New York City. Her father was a successful sugar merchant. He gave his seven children a good education. They learned at home from private tutors. Lazarus studied literature and music. She learned French, German, and Italian. She also loved to write. Her father published her first book of poems in 1866. She was 17 years old.

Lazarus published a second book of poems in 1871. The title was *Admetus and Other Poems*. The *Illustrated London News* called her "a poet of rare original power."[2] She became a successful poet.

Lazarus wrote magazine articles as well. Some of her articles discussed American literature. She wanted American authors to write in a new voice. She didn't want them to copy European style. She praised writers such as Nathaniel Hawthorne, Walt Whitman, and Harriet Beecher Stowe.

Lazarus also translated works from German. In 1881, she published *Poems and Ballads of Heinrich Heine*. Heine was a famous German Jewish poet. Many writers praised her work. *The Critic* said that it was "made by an artist's hand."[3]

At this time, anti-Semitism was rising in Europe. Hatred of Jews made life hard for many Jewish people. The problem was especially bad in Russia. Organized government gangs attacked Jewish villages. They killed many people. Many Russian Jews escaped to the United States.

Between 1880 and 1920, the United States received a flood of immigrants. More than 20 million people arrived in the country. Before 1900, most immigrants came from northwestern Europe. Later, more immigrants came from southern and eastern Europe. Jews fleeing violence in Russia were part of this flood.

In the 1880s, Lazarus volunteered to help Russian Jewish immigrants. She worked for the Hebrew Emigrant Aid

Society. She visited with immigrants. Many were poor and unskilled. She worried about their futures. She helped to set up the Hebrew Technical Institute. This school trained immigrants for jobs.

Lazarus's work with Russian Jews changed her life. She began to study more about her own Jewish culture. She worked hard to learn Hebrew. She wrote more often on Jewish topics. She spoke out against anti-Semitism in the United States and Europe.

In 1882, Lazarus published *Songs of a Semite*. Many people think that it is her best work. It includes a play and poems with Jewish themes.

During this same time, Lazarus also supported the work of the Franco-American Union. This group included people in France and the United States. The group planned to build a statue in New York Harbor. The statue would honor U.S. liberty. French artists and workers created the statue. But Americans had to build a base, or pedestal, for it.

To raise money, the Franco-American Union held an auction. Well-known authors wrote about the Statue of Liberty. The group sold these works at the auction. Lazarus wrote a poem called "The New Colossus." (*Colossus* means "giant.") Her poem welcomed immigrants to the United States.

The pedestal was completed in 1886. Then the Statue of Liberty was set up in New York Harbor. It still stands there today. Many thousands of people see the statue each year.

Lazarus died of cancer on November 19, 1887. She was just 38 years old. But 16 years after her death, her poem was placed on the pedestal of the Statue of Liberty. Now new immigrants can read her words of welcome there. They can remember Emma Lazarus.

Ellis Island is in New York Harbor, in the shadow of the Statue of Liberty. Between 1892 and 1954, more than 12 million immigrants entered the United States at Ellis Island. Today, two out of every five Americans can trace their families to someone who arrived there.[4]

Comprehension

Check the correct answer.

1. When she was a child, Lazarus

    _____ a. went to the best schools.

    _____ b. learned at home from tutors.

2. Lazarus's first book of poems was published

    _____ a. when she was 17 years old.

    _____ b. when she was 38 years old.

3. Lazarus thought that American writers

    _____ a. should copy the best European styles.

    _____ b. should write in an American style.

4. In the 1880s, many Russian Jews came to the United States

    _____ a. to escape anti-Semitism in Russia.

    _____ b. to become prosperous merchants.

5. Lazarus became more interested in Jewish culture when

    _____ a. she read books about it.

    _____ b. she helped Russian Jewish immigrants.

6. France gave the Statue of Liberty to the United States, but the United States had to

    _____ a. build a pedestal.

    _____ b. ship it across the Atlantic.

7. "The New Colossus"

    _____ a. was about Jewish themes.

    _____ b. welcomed immigrants to the United States.

Sequence

Work with a partner. Number the events in the correct order.

_____ "The New Colossus" is placed on the pedestal of
the Statue of Liberty.

_____ Lazarus dies at age 38.

_____ Lazarus begins helping Russian Jewish immigrants.

_____ Lazarus studies French, German, and Italian.

_____ Lazarus becomes more interested in Jewish culture.

Vocabulary

Look at these words from the reading. Put a check next to words that
you know. Underline words that you don't know yet. Find the words in
the reading. Try to guess their meanings.

ancestors	auction	merchant	themes
anti-Semitism	literature	pedestal	volunteer

Use the words to fill in the blanks in the sentences.

1. Your _____ include your grandparents' parents and

   their parents.

2. Lazarus's father was a _____ who bought and sold sugar.

3. Good novels, poems, and short stories are examples of _____.

4. Hating Jews is called _____.

5. When you _____ to work, you don't get paid for it.

6. Lazarus wrote about Jewish _____, or topics and ideas.

7. Lazarus's poem was placed on the Statue of Liberty's _____.

8. Selling items at an _____ is a way to raise money.

Reading a Chart

A chart is a useful way to organize facts. This chart shows facts about immigration to the United States. Before 1900, most immigrants came from northwestern and central Europe. However, after 1900, more and more immigrants came from eastern and southern Europe.

Immigration Table[5]

Years	From Northwestern and Central Europe	% of Total	From Eastern and Southern Europe	% of Total	Total Immigrants from All Countries
1891–1895	1,508,000	71%	566,000	27%	2,124,000
1896–1900	825,000	53%	660,000	42%	1,564,000
1901–1905	1,883,000	49%	1,762,000	46%	3,833,000
1906–1910	2,173,000	44%	2,318,000	47%	4,962,000

Fill in the blanks. Use information from the table.

1. In the years 1906–1910, _____ immigrants came from eastern and southern Europe.

2. In the years 1891–1895, _____ immigrants came from northwestern and central Europe. However, in the years 1896–1900, _____ immigrants came from northwestern and central Europe.

3. The largest number of total immigrants came in the years _____.

4. The number of immigrants from eastern and southern Europe was more than the number from northwestern and central Europe in the years _____.

5. Immigrants from northwestern and central Europe were less than half of total immigrants in the years _____ and _____.

If the Statue of Liberty could talk, what do you think she would say?

Connecting Today and Yesterday

1. Did you ever visit the Statue of Liberty? If yes, what did you think?

2. Are there any statues in your neighborhood or city? If so, why were they built?

Group Activity

Find a picture of the Statue of Liberty. Share it with your group. Then discuss these questions.

1. Why is the statue a woman?

2. Why is she holding a torch?

3. Why is she holding a stone tablet with the date 1776?

4. Why is there a broken chain around her feet?

Class Discussion

1. Why is the Statue of Liberty important to Americans?

2. The United States is sometimes called "a nation of nations." Why?

3. How did Lazarus become more interested in her own Jewish culture? Did this ever happen to you or someone you know?

Reflections

1. What was the most interesting thing that you read in this lesson?

2. How can you learn more about Emma Lazarus or the Statue of Liberty?

Woody Guthrie

"If you look hard enough you can see plenty to sing about."
—*Woody Guthrie*[1]

Pre-Reading Questions

1. Read the words under the title. What do you think that they mean?

2. Can music express beliefs? Can a song affect history? Explain your opinions.

Reading Preview

Woody Guthrie was a folksinger and songwriter. He wrote songs about ordinary Americans and the need to respect everyone.

Woody Guthrie

In the United States in the 1930s, many farmers had problems. There was an economic depression. Many farmers couldn't pay their mortgages. They lost their land. At the same time, there was a seven-year drought. The worst area was called the Dust Bowl. The soil dried up and blew away. Whole families became migrant workers. They traveled to California and Arizona looking for work. Living conditions were harsh. Their pay was small.

But Woody Guthrie wanted to change that. He was a songwriter and musician. He wrote songs about the migrants' hard lives. He sang them on the radio and at meetings around the country. Soon Guthrie's music and guitar became the migrants' voice.

Woody Guthrie was born in 1912 in Okemah, Oklahoma. His father owned a successful real estate business. His parents played piano and sang spirituals and ballads. These songs were passed from one generation to another. The songs were often religious or told melancholy—sad—stories about the simple country life. Guthrie showed a great talent for music. He learned the songs that his parents taught him. He easily learned to play harmonica.

But Guthrie also knew tragedy when he was a child. The family's new house burned down. Guthrie's father went broke. Guthrie's sister Clara died in another fire. His mother became erratic. She behaved strangely and was sometimes violent. She had to go into the state mental hospital. She later died there. She had Huntington's chorea, but no one knew it at the time. This is a genetic disease that destroys the nervous system. It can be passed from parents to children.

Guthrie's father moved to Pampas, Texas, to live with his sister. But Guthrie and his oldest brother stayed in Okemah. Guthrie moved in and out of different families. Sometimes he lived on the street. He made money by singing and playing the harmonica. He played music for dances. He also painted signs. In 1929, he went to live in Texas with his father. There his uncle taught him to play the guitar. He also met his first wife, Mary. They married in 1933.

In Texas, Guthrie saw dust storms destroy farmland. He saw jobless men and their hungry families on the side of the road. He left Texas, and he rode the railroads west. He sang in migrant camps. Many of the migrants came from the same area as he did. They asked him to sing the ballads they remembered from their childhood. When Guthrie sang, tears filled their eyes. Guthrie realized that his music was more than entertainment. He was singing their past. These people had lost everything. All they had left was the music.

Guthrie was a prolific songwriter. He wrote many songs about these "Dust Bowl refugees."

In 1940, Guthrie moved to New York. He got a recording contract. He became famous and successful. He also recorded music for the Archive of American Folk Song at the Library of Congress. This collection of folk songs shows American heritage and culture. Guthrie later joined the Almanac Singers. They played at union meetings and for farm and workers groups.

In 1942, Guthrie fell in love with a dancer named Marjorie Mazia. They had a child together. They divorced their spouses and married in 1945. In 1947, Guthrie had another tragedy. Cathy Ann, his child with Marjorie, died in an electrical fire. In time, they had three more children.

In the late 1940s, Guthrie's health began to deteriorate. He couldn't concentrate. His behavior became erratic. In 1952, doctors finally discovered the problem. He had Huntington's Chorea. It was the same genetic illness that his mother had. In 1956, he was put in a mental hospital.

Guthrie gradually lost the ability to play the guitar and to write. But he still influenced music. Many young musicians visited him. Some, like Bob Dylan, went on to become famous themselves.

But Guthrie's condition continued to deteriorate. By 1965, he could no longer speak. He died on October 3, 1967.

Guthrie's music had a big impact on U.S. culture. His songs show a great love and understanding of the life of common people. His legacy continues with the Woody Guthrie Foundation and Archives. This organization has the largest collection of his work in the world.

The Almanac Singers was one of the first popular folk music groups in the United States. The group included Guthrie and two other famous songwriters and singers, Pete Seeger and Lee Hays.

Comprehension

Complete the sentences. Use information from the reading.

1. In the 1930s, part of the country was called "the Dust Bowl" because _____

   _____

   _____.

2. When Guthrie was young, he learned about music from _____

   _____

   _____.

3. Huntington's chorea is _____

   _____.

4. After his father moved to Texas, Guthrie made money by _____

   _____

   _____.

5. When Guthrie sang songs that the migrants remembered, they _____

   _____

   _____.

6. After Guthrie moved to New York, he _____

   _____

   _____.

7. The Archive of American Folk Song is _____

   _____.

Fact or Opinion

Work with a partner. Decide if each sentence is a fact or an opinion. Then write *F* for *fact* or *O* for *opinion* in front of each sentence.

_____ 1. During the 1930s, migrant workers traveled west to California and Arizona.

_____ 2. Guthrie's father was wrong to move to Texas and leave Guthrie and his brother in Oklahoma.

_____ 3. It was unfair that Guthrie had so much tragedy in his life.

_____ 4. Guthrie died from the same disease that his mother had.

_____ 5. Guthrie's music is a valuable part of the Archive of American Folk Song.

Vocabulary

Look at these words from the reading. Put a check next to words that you know. Underline words that you don't know yet. Find the words in the reading. Try to guess their meanings.

ballad	erratic	genetic	prolific
deteriorate	generation	melancholy	refugee

Match each word with its definition.

_____ 1. ballad   a. all the people born at about the same time

_____ 2. generation   b. not making sense; changing in odd ways

_____ 3. melancholy   c. sad

_____ 4. erratic   d. folk song that tells a story

_____ 5. genetic   e. person who leaves home to escape danger

_____ 6. prolific   f. passed from parents to children

_____ 7. refugee   g. to get worse

_____ 8. deteriorate   h. producing a lot of work

Reading a Map

Physical maps show features of the land and water. **Political maps** show borders between countries, states, or other political regions. **Road maps** show roads, highways, and other travel information. Many maps, like this one, combine all three types. It shows physical features and states in the United States. It also shows Route 66. This highway made it easier for migrant workers to travel west.

Route 66: The Path of the Migrant Workers

Answer the questions. Use information from the map.

1. How many states does Route 66 go through? What are they? _____

   _____

2. In which states does Route 66 go from northeast to southwest? _____

   _____

3. In which states does Route 66 go from east to west? _____

   _____

4. In which part of California is Route 66? _____

5. Why did migrant workers go to this part of California? _____

Connecting Today and Yesterday

1. Woody Guthrie used his music to improve the lives of migrant workers. Do any artists today use their art to change people's lives? Discuss any that you know about.

2. Guthrie's family taught him songs that were passed from one generation to another. Do families still teach this kind of song? Do you think teaching them is important? Why or why not?

Group Activities

1. Find a recording of Woody Guthrie's song "This Land Is Your Land." With your group, listen to the words and the music. Then answer these questions.

   • What is Guthrie's attitude toward the land?

   • Does the song reflect the U.S. spirit? If so, how?

   • Does the song express any political views?

2. Watch the film *The Grapes of Wrath.* Discuss it with your group. What did you learn about the Dust Bowl refugees? What was interesting? What was surprising?

Class Discussion

1. Why were the migrant workers of the 1930s called "Dust Bowl refugees"?

2. Guthrie wrote, "A folk song ought to be pretty well satisfied just to tell the facts and let it go at that."[2] In what ways did his music do that?

3. Do you think Guthrie's music was influenced by the tragedies in his life? Explain. Does tragedy affect a person's art? Why or why not?

Reflections

1. What was the most interesting thing that you read in this lesson?

2. Can you use anything from Woody Guthrie's story in your own life? Explain.

Woody Guthrie said, "All you can write is what you see."[3]

What did he mean by that?

Helen Keller

"Keep your face to the sunshine and you cannot see the shadow."

—Helen Keller[1]

Pre-Reading Questions

1. Read the words under the title. What do you think that they mean? Do you agree or disagree? Explain.

2. When you have trouble, do you "keep your face to the sunshine"? What happens?

Reading Preview

Helen Keller was deaf and blind. Her active, courageous life changed the image of disabled people. She worked for better education and living conditions for disabled people.

Helen Keller

Helen Keller was born in 1880 in Tuscumbia, Alabama. When she was a baby, she could see and hear. But at 19 months old, she had a high fever. At first, doctors thought that she might die. Then the fever passed.

But her mother noticed something wrong. When she rang the dinner bell, Helen didn't react. When she passed her hand in front of Helen's eyes, Helen didn't respond. Because of the fever, Helen was deaf and blind.

Without sight and hearing, Keller was frustrated. Her behavior was hard to control. She angrily smashed dishes and lamps. She screamed and had temper tantrums.

When Keller was 6 years old, her parents asked Alexander Graham Bell for advice. Bell is famous for inventing the telephone. But he was also a teacher of deaf children. Bell suggested that they ask Michael Anagnos to recommend a teacher. Anagnos was director of the Perkins Institution for the Blind. He recommended Anne Sullivan. Sullivan, a top student, graduated that year. Her eyesight was poor, but she wasn't blind. Sullivan agreed to become Keller's private teacher.

Sullivan had a lot of patience. She had to teach Keller what language was. She started with the manual, or hand, alphabet. This alphabet uses simple finger signs for letters. She spelled words into Helen's palm. Soon Keller learned what words meant and how to use them.

Keller was elated when she could communicate. Her progress was astonishing. Quickly she learned to read raised letters and then Braille. Braille uses raised dots for letters. Sullivan also taught Keller how to use a Braille typewriter and a regular typewriter.

In 1889, Keller and Sullivan moved to the Perkins Institution. Sullivan went to classes with Keller. She used the manual alphabet to spell lessons into Keller's hand. Then in 1894, they moved to New York City to study at the new Wright-Humason School for the Deaf. They lived near Central Park. Sullivan taught Keller how to ride horses. They rode horses daily through the park.

In New York, they met Mark Twain. Twain thought that Keller was remarkable. He once said, "The two most interesting characters of the 19th century are Napoleon and Helen Keller."[2] He was fascinated by the relationship between Sullivan and Keller. He believed that they were so close that their personalities merged into one person.

In 1896, Keller and Sullivan moved to Boston so that Keller could prepare for college. Keller attended the Cambridge School for Young Ladies. She studied history, math, literature, and physics. Then she was accepted at Radcliffe College and began classes there in 1900. Radcliffe was one of the best women's colleges in the United States. Only top students were accepted. In 1904, Keller became the first deaf-blind person to earn a bachelor's degree. She graduated with honors.

In Boston, Sullivan and Keller met John Macy. Macy edited Keller's first book, *The Story of My Life.* He also influenced her politics. Keller began to support voting rights for women. She also became a socialist. Socialism is an economic system. In socialism, the whole society owns the companies that make and distribute goods. In theory, people cooperate instead of competing for profit. Macy and Sullivan married in 1905.

In later years, Keller traveled to raise money for the American Foundation for the Blind. She supported better education and jobs for disabled people. Anne Sullivan Macy died in 1936. But Keller continued her travels with her secretary, Polly Thompson.

In 1957, the play *The Miracle Worker* opened. It told Keller's story. Later it became a movie. The well-known actress Anne Bancroft played Sullivan. And the young Patty Duke played Keller. Both women won Academy Awards.

In 1964, President Lyndon Johnson gave Helen Keller the Presidential Medal of Freedom. It is the highest civilian award in the United States.

Keller died in 1968. She was 88 years old. Through her work, millions learned that disabled people are people like everyone else.

Comprehension

Check the correct answer.

1. When Keller was born,

    _____ a. she was deaf and blind.

    _____ b. she could see and hear.

2. Keller's parents thought that Alexander Graham Bell could help them because

    _____ a. he was a teacher of deaf children.

    _____ b. he was an expert in technology for the blind.

3. When Keller attended classes,

    _____ a. she always went alone.

    _____ b. Anne Sullivan always went with her.

4. Keller attended the Cambridge School for Young Ladies

    _____ a. to prepare for college.

    _____ b. to learn social skills.

5. In theory, in socialism,

    _____ a. people cooperate.

    _____ b. people compete for profits.

6. Keller raised money

    _____ a. for the American Federation for the Blind.

    _____ b. to pay for her education.

7. The Presidential Medal of Freedom

    _____ a. is the highest U.S. military honor.

    _____ b. is the highest U.S. civilian honor.

Helen Keller met many famous people. She once said that she met every U.S. president from Grover Cleveland to John F. Kennedy.[3]

Sequence

Work with a partner. Number the events in the correct order.

_____ Keller publishes *The Story of My Life.*

_____ The Keller family goes to see Alexander Graham Bell.

_____ Keller receives the Presidential Medal of Freedom.

_____ Keller meets Mark Twain.

_____ *The Miracle Worker* opens.

Vocabulary

Look at these words from the reading. Put a check next to words that you know. Underline words that you don't know yet. Find the words in the reading. Try to guess their meanings.

astonishing	elated	manual	socialism
civilian	frustrated	recommend	temper tantrums

Use the words to fill in the blanks in the sentences.

1. When Keller was _____, she became angry.

2. Keller's _____ made her family's life difficult.

3. The Kellers asked Michael Anagnos to _____ a teacher, and he suggested Anne Sullivan.

4. When you use the _____ alphabet, you use your hands to make letters.

5. Keller was excited and _____ when she learned to communicate with the manual alphabet.

6. It was _____ that Keller learned so quickly.

7. _____ is an economic system.

8. A _____ is a person who is not in the military.

Reading a Time Line

A time line shows dates and events in order on a line.

Helen Keller's Life

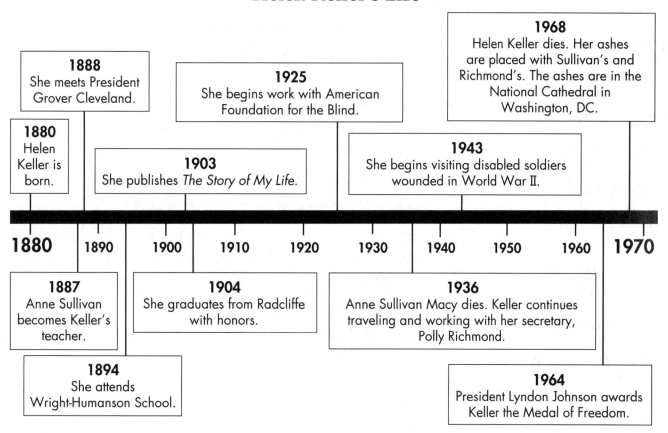

Answer the questions. Use information from the time line.

1. Anne Sullivan stayed with Keller for how many years? _____

2. Who was the first U.S. president that Keller met? _____

3. Which president gave Keller the Medal of Freedom? _____

4. What did Keller do during World War II? _____

_____

5. Where are Keller's ashes buried? _____

6. Who else is buried with her? _____

Helen Keller wrote, "I . . . can give one hint to those who see. . . . Use your eyes as if tomorrow you would be stricken blind."[4]

What did she mean? Do you think that it is good advice?

Connecting Today and Yesterday

1. When Keller was a child, many blind and deaf children didn't go to school. How have things changed today?

2. In Keller's time, people with disabilities usually didn't marry. People thought that they shouldn't have children. Have ideas changed today? What do you think?

Group Activities

1. Watch the film *The Miracle Worker*. Then discuss these questions with your group.

   - When did Keller first understand that Sullivan's finger movements were a way to communicate?

   - Describe the relationship between Sullivan and Keller. When was it positive? When was it negative? Give examples.

   - What did you learn from this film? What surprised you? Has it changed any of your ideas about blind and deaf people? Explain.

2. Research Alexander Graham Bell's interest in teaching deaf people. Then discuss it in your group. How did it help him invent the telephone?

Class Discussion

1. Was the close relationship between Keller and Sullivan good or bad for Keller? For Sullivan? Do you think that Keller would have been able to succeed without Sullivan?

2. In what ways was Keller a model for disabled people?

3. How would your life change if you suddenly became blind and deaf? How would it affect your family, your work, and your goals?

Reflections

1. What was the most interesting thing that you read in this lesson?

2. How can you learn more about Helen Keller or the rights of disabled people?

Jackie Robinson

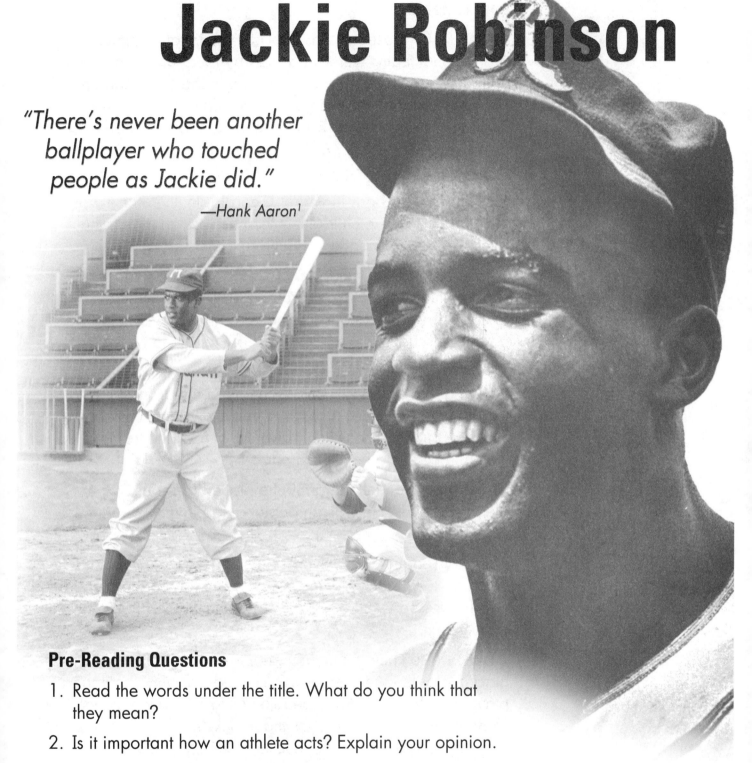

"There's never been another ballplayer who touched people as Jackie did."

—Hank Aaron[1]

Pre-Reading Questions

1. Read the words under the title. What do you think that they mean?

2. Is it important how an athlete acts? Explain your opinion.

Reading Preview

Jackie Robinson was the first black player in baseball's major leagues in the 20th century. He faced abuse and harassment. His skill, courage, and endurance inspired many Americans. And he opened the door for more black athletes.

Jackie Robinson

In the 1940s, baseball was the U.S. "national pastime." But professional teams were separated by race. Blacks played in the Negro Leagues. Whites played in the American and National Leagues—the major leagues. In 1947, Jackie Robinson changed that. He joined the National League's Brooklyn Dodgers. He was the first black player to cross baseball's color line in the 20th century.

Robinson was born in Cairo, Georgia, in 1919. He was the youngest of five children. When he was an infant, the family moved to Pasadena, California.

Robinson showed an amazing ability to excel at any sport. In high school, he starred on four teams. He played football, baseball, and basketball, and he ran track. He won a football scholarship to UCLA. But he had to leave college early to help support his mother.

During World War II, Robinson joined the army. At first, the army told him that a black man couldn't attend officer training. But Robinson didn't give up. He got the training. In time he became a first lieutenant.

After Robinson left the army, he played baseball in the Negro Leagues. He was an outstanding player.

At that time, Branch Rickey was general manager of the National League's Brooklyn Dodgers. Rickey knew that it was unfair to keep black players out of the major leagues. And he was impressed with Robinson's skills. He wanted Robinson on his team.

Rickey also knew that many people would insult the first black major leaguer. Some would try to hurt him. But if the player fought back, many people would blame the player. They would say, "This proves that blacks and whites can't play baseball together." To succeed, Rickey thought, the player had to hold his temper.

Rickey met with Robinson. He asked if Robinson could stay calm when people mistreated him. He asked Robinson not to fight back for two years. It was a difficult decision. But finally Robinson agreed. Rickey hired him. Robinson played one season for the minor league Montreal team. Then in April 1947, he joined the Brooklyn Dodgers.

Robinson had problems right away. Some fans cheered him, but others yelled racial taunts. People threw things onto the field. Often, opposing players deliberately tried to hurt or upset him. Pitchers threw balls at his head. Base runners slid into him. Catchers spit on his shoes.

There were more problems when the Dodgers traveled. Some hotels wouldn't rent Robinson a room. Some restaurants refused to serve him. In Philadelphia, the Phillies manager shouted racial slurs. Robinson got hate mail and even death threats.

These problems angered Robinson. But he was strong enough to stay calm. He kept his promise to Rickey. And through it all, he played outstanding baseball. He was very competitive. He was a daring base runner, a skillful fielder, and an excellent hitter. *Sporting News* named him the 1947 "Rookie of the Year."

Robinson played 10 seasons for the Dodgers. And he kept playing excellent baseball. He was famous for stealing bases. He stole home 19 times—once in the 1955 World Series. In 1949, he was the National League's Most Valuable Player.

Robinson retired from baseball in 1956, at age 37. In 1962, he was elected to baseball's Hall of Fame. That was the first year that he was eligible.

Robinson's success was an inspiration to many Americans, especially blacks. Historian Roger Wilkins, who is black, was 15 years old in 1947. Wilkins didn't know Robinson personally, but he felt close to him. He felt Robinson "was carrying me right on his shoulders."[2]

All over the country, black preachers asked their congregations to pray for Robinson's success. There were Jackie Robinson movies, songs, and even comic books.

Robinson's courage helped integrate baseball. Soon more black players were playing in the major leagues. By 1959, all the teams were integrated.

After retiring, Robinson continued his work for racial justice. He demanded that major league baseball hire

The Brooklyn Dodgers were the best team in the National League for 6 of the 10 years that Robinson played with them. He helped them win six pennants and one World Series.

black managers and coaches. He worked for the NAACP (National Association for the Advancement of Colored People). He wrote to government officials about civil rights.

Jackie Robinson died of a heart attack in 1972. He is remembered for his courage, dignity, and skill.

Comprehension

Complete the sentences. Use information from the reading.

1. Robinson showed that he was a outstanding athlete in school by _____

_____.

2. In the army, Robinson _____

_____.

3. Rickey wanted Robinson on the Brooklyn Dodgers because _____

_____.

4. For Robinson's first two years with the Dodgers, Rickey wanted him to _____

_____.

5. When Robinson played, opposing players _____

_____.

6. While he was a Dodger, some of Robinson's successes were _____

_____.

7. After he retired, Robinson _____

_____.

Fact or Opinion

Work with a partner. Decide if each sentence is a fact or an opinion. Then write *F* for *fact* or *O* for *opinion* in front of each sentence.

_____ 1. Integrating major league baseball was Robinson's most important success.

_____ 2. Abuse from the Phillies manager was the worst racism that Robinson faced.

_____ 3. When Robinson played for the Dodgers, many people mistreated him.

_____ 4. Many black people identified with Robinson's success.

Vocabulary

Look at these words from the reading. Put a check next to words that you know. Underline words that you don't know yet. Find the words in the reading. Try to guess their meanings.

competitive congregation	daring deliberately	eligible integrate	taunt threat

Match each word with its definition.

_____ 1. taunt

_____ 2. deliberately

_____ 3. threat

_____ 4. competitive

_____ 5. daring

_____ 6. eligible

_____ 7. congregation

_____ 8. integrate

a. liking to win

b. taking risks; brave

c. people gathered for worship

d. an insult

e. on purpose; not by accident

f. to open something to people of all races

g. allowed to be chosen

h. a warning; words saying that the speaker means to hurt someone

Reading a Chart

A chart is a useful way to organize facts.

Three Early Black Major Leaguers[3]

Player	In Major Leagues	Career Highlights
Larry Doby	1947–1959	• second player to integrate a major league team, first in the American League • played in seven All-Star games • second black major league manager • entered Baseball Hall of Fame in 1998
Roy Campanella	1948–1957	• set records for fielding and hitting by a catcher • three times National League MVP* • career ended by car accident in 1958 • entered Baseball Hall of Fame in 1969
Hank Aaron	1954–1976	• hit 755 home runs (the all-time record) • played in 24 All-Star games • 1957 National League MVP* • entered Baseball Hall of Fame in 1982

*MVP: most valuable player

Answer the questions. Use information from the chart.

1. Who was the second black player to join an all-white team? _____

   What year was he hired? _____

2. What was Roy Campanella's last season playing baseball? _____

   What ended his career? _____

3. How many home runs did Hank Aaron hit? _____

4. Which of these players were All-Stars? _____

5. Which of these players won the Most Valuable Player award? _____

   _____

6. Which of these players are in the Baseball Hall of Fame? _____

   _____

Connecting Today and Yesterday

1. Integrated sports teams were rare in the 1940s. Are all teams integrated today? What roles do black players have in major sports today?

2. For many years, baseball was the most popular sport in the United States. What sports are most popular today? Is baseball still an important part of U.S. culture?

Group Activity

When Jackie Robinson joined the Dodgers, it was national news. Look up newspaper and magazine reports for November 25, 1945 (the day that Rickey hired Robinson) and for April 15, 1947 (Robinson's first day playing with the Dodgers). Bring in information to share with your group. Discuss these questions.

1. Which stories were positive? Which stories were negative?

2. Why did Robinson get so much attention?

3. Would you have gone to his first game? Why or why not?

Class Discussion

1. What did Robinson's success mean to black Americans?

2. Why did Rickey ask Robinson not to fight back for the first two years? Was it a good idea? Why or why not?

3. Robinson knew that he would face many problems when he joined the Dodgers. Talk about your opinions on these questions: Why did he decide to do it? Did he ever regret his decision? How would you react to the same problems?

Reflections

1. What was the most interesting thing that you read in this lesson?

2. How can you learn more about Jackie Robinson or baseball?

NBA superstar Charles Barkley said that Robinson "probably was the single most important black athlete who's ever lived." He also called Robinson "one of the greatest black men who's ever lived."[4]

Why did he say that? Explain your opinion.

John F. Kennedy

"The stories of past courage . . . can teach, they can offer hope, they can provide inspiration. But they cannot supply courage itself. For this each man must look into his own soul."

—John F. Kennedy

Pre-Reading Questions

1. Read the words under the title. What do you think that they mean? Do you agree or disagree? Explain.

2. Are people born with courage, or do they develop it? When have you needed courage?

Reading Preview

John F. Kennedy was a popular U.S. president. He showed courage in many difficult times. And he worked for the ideals of freedom and equality. The world was shocked when he was assassinated.

John F. Kennedy

John F. Kennedy was president at a troubled time. At home, blacks were demanding equal rights. Abroad, the Cold War between the Soviet Union and the United States was heating up. While Kennedy was in office, these two countries came to the brink of nuclear war.

Kennedy was born on May 29, 1917, in Brookline, Massachusetts. He was the second of nine children. As a teenager, Kennedy attended Choate Academy, a prep school in Connecticut.

After Choate, Kennedy started at Princeton. But soon he became ill and had to drop out. Later, he went to Harvard. There, he hurt his back playing football. He had back pain for the rest of his life.

Soon after college, Kennedy joined the Navy. In 1941, the United States entered World War II. Kennedy was sent to the South Pacific. He commanded a small patrol boat called *PT-109*. In August 1943, an enemy warship rammed his boat. Two men died. But Kennedy saved the rest of his crew. He received a medal for courage.

After the war, Kennedy had to pick a career. His family had a history of public service. His grandfather was mayor of Boston. His father was once ambassador to England. Kennedy discussed careers with his father. His father suggested politics.

So in 1946, Kennedy ran for Congress. He won. He served six years as a Congressman from Massachusetts. Then in 1952, he was elected U.S. Senator. The next year, he married Jacqueline Bouvier. In their early years together, he had two dangerous back surgeries. During his convalescence, he wrote a book called *Profiles in Courage*. In 1957, it won the Pulitzer Prize.

Kennedy was a popular politician. In 1960, he ran for president against Richard Nixon. The candidates debated on TV. It was the first time TV showed a debate with candidates for president. Kennedy looked confident and handsome. Viewers were impressed. He won the election by a small margin. At 43, he was the youngest U.S. president ever elected. He was also the first Roman Catholic president.

Kennedy brought a youthful spirit to the United States. He wanted to inspire young people to serve their country. He created the Peace Corps. This agency sends U.S. volunteers to work in developing countries. He also supported exploring space. In 1961, Kennedy said that the United States would land a man on the moon. He said it would happen by 1970. And in 1969, U.S. astronaut Neil Armstrong walked on the moon.

In foreign policy, Kennedy's biggest challenge came from the Soviet Union. The United States and Soviet Union were rivals. They were also both superpowers. One serious event happened in October 1962. U.S. planes detected Soviet missiles in Cuba. Cuba is only 90 miles from the United States. Kennedy and his advisers talked about what to do. Then Kennedy took a brave and risky step. He announced a blockade of Cuba. The U.S. Navy would not let ships in or out of Cuba. The world feared nuclear war. Secret talks began. The Soviets agreed to take away the missiles. And the United States promised not to invade Cuba. After one week, the Cuban Missile Crisis ended.

Kennedy also faced challenges in Vietnam. North Vietnam was fighting the government of South Vietnam. North Vietnam's government was Communist. Kennedy believed that the United States had to stop Communism. He sent U.S. advisers to support South Vietnam. Later in the 1960s, the United States sent combat troops. It became involved in the Vietnam War.

At home, the civil rights movement was winning court cases. Kennedy supported existing laws. But at first, he didn't suggest new laws to protect civil rights. Then in May 1963, TV showed police attacking peaceful protestors in Birmingham, Alabama. Kennedy was forced to act. He announced that he would ask for new civil rights laws. But Kennedy died before the laws passed. He was assassinated November 22, 1963, in Dallas, Texas.

People around the world mourned. Kennedy was president for only three years. But he showed courage in many ways. And he inspired the nation.

Comprehension

Check the correct answer.

1. Kennedy faced many challenges
   _____ a. at home and abroad.
   _____ b. mainly at home in the United States.

2. When *PT-109* was attacked,
   _____ a. all the crewmen were killed.
   _____ b. two men died, but Kennedy saved the rest.

3. Kennedy entered politics because
   _____ a. his father suggested it.
   _____ b. he wanted to be president.

4. Kennedy wrote *Profiles in Courage*
   _____ a. before he got married.
   _____ b. after his back surgeries.

5. The United States sent men to the moon
   _____ a. sooner than Kennedy said.
   _____ b. later than Kennedy said.

6. After the United States detected Soviet missiles in Cuba,
   _____ a. Kennedy announced a blockade of Cuba.
   _____ b. Kennedy sent U.S. troops to Cuba.

7. Kennedy was president
   _____ a. for eight years.
   _____ b. for three years.

"This nation . . . will not be fully free until all its citizens are free."

—John F. Kennedy[2]

Sequence

Work with a partner. Number the events in the correct order.

_____ Kennedy commands *PT-109*.

_____ Kennedy orders the blockade of Cuba.

_____ Kennedy writes *Profiles in Courage*.

_____ Kennedy attends Harvard.

_____ Kennedy supports new civil rights laws.

Vocabulary

Look at these words from the reading. Put a check next to words that you know. Underline words that you don't know yet. Find the words in the reading. Try to guess their meanings.

blockade	commanded	detected	prep school
brink	convalescence	inspire	rivals

Use the words to fill in the blanks in the sentences.

1. In October 1962, the world was on the _____ of nuclear war.

2. A _____ prepares students for college.

3. When Kennedy _____ a patrol boat, he had to take care of his crew.

4. After back surgery, during his _____, Kennedy wrote *Profiles in Courage*.

5. Kennedy tried to _____ the nation, especially young people.

6. Because the United States and the Soviet Union were _____, relations between them were often dangerous.

7. Kennedy was worried when the United States _____ Soviet missiles in Cuba.

8. Kennedy ordered a _____ of ships going in or out of Cuba.

Reading a Time Line

A time line shows dates and events in order on a line.

John F. Kennedy's Life

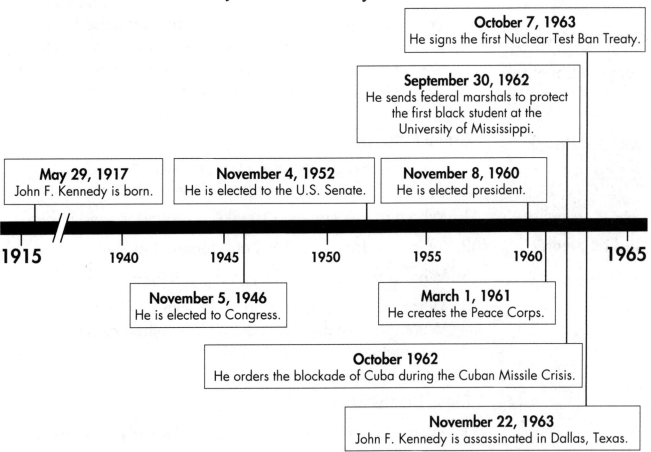

Answer the questions. Use information from the time line.

1. How many elected offices did Kennedy hold? _____

2. Was the Peace Corps created at the beginning or the

   end of Kennedy's term? _____

3. What treaty reduced testing of nuclear weapons? _____

   When did Kennedy sign it? _____

4. How old was Kennedy when he died? _____

5. Which event was Kennedy's biggest challenge? Explain

   why you think so. _____

Kennedy said, "Ask not what your country can do for you—ask what you can do for your country."[3]

What did he mean?

Connecting Today and Yesterday

1. Kennedy wanted to stop Communism. Is Communism a threat to the United States today? What are the biggest problems in U.S. foreign policy today? Explain.

2. When Kennedy was president, his brother Robert was U.S. Attorney General. His brother Edward was elected senator from Massachusetts. Do any political families hold several high offices today? If yes, who are they?

Group Activity

Some people still argue about who killed Kennedy. Research his murder. Bring information to your group. Then discuss these questions.

1. Who was Lee Harvey Oswald? What happened to him?

2. Who was Jack Ruby? What happened to him?

3. What is the Zapruder film? Why is it important?

4. What groups have investigated Kennedy's murder? What did they decide about it? Were their decisions reasonable?

Class Discussion

1. Would things be different today if Kennedy wasn't killed? If yes, how? Explain your opinion.

2. Kennedy had Addison's Disease. This illness affects a person's immune system. He also had back pain. He had to take a lot of medicine. But most Americans didn't know about his health problems. Should the public know about the president's health? Why or why not?

Reflections

1. What was the most interesting thing that you read in this lesson?

2. How can you learn more about John F. Kennedy or the 1960s?

Sandra Cisneros

"She is nobody's mother and nobody's wife."

—Sandra Cisneros, describing herself[1]

Sandra Cisneros

The House on Mango Street

"Sandra Cisneros is one of the most brilliant of today's young writers. Her work is sensitive, alert, nuanceful... rich with music and picture."—Gwendolyn Brooks

Pre-Reading Questions

1. Read the words under the title. What do you think that they mean? Do you think Cisneros feels proud or sad when she says this? Explain.

2. Have you ever learned about someone else's culture from stories or poems? If yes, describe what you learned.

Reading Preview

Sandra Cisneros is a popular Mexican American writer. She writes stories about Chicano culture and about strong women. Many U.S. schools use her book *The House on Mango Street.*

Sandra Cisneros

In recent years, a new Chicano literature has emerged. It expresses pride in Mexican culture. It explores the conflicts of living in two cultures at one time. It also looks at the cultural roles of men and women. One of the first writers to write about these themes was Sandra Cisneros.

Cisneros was born in 1954 in Chicago. Her father was from Mexico, and her mother was Mexican American. Spanish was her first language. Cisneros's family was poor. They often moved between Mexico City and Chicago. They never stayed in one place long enough to feel settled.

These constant changes upset Cisneros. She became introverted and shy. She had few friends.

Although the family was poor, her parents valued education. Her mother made sure that Cisneros and her six brothers each had a library card. The house was full of borrowed books. Cisneros was an avid reader. She enjoyed the world of imagination inside books.

Cisneros went to Catholic grade schools. She began writing poems in elementary school. But she kept them private. She didn't feel confident. But when she was in high school, one of her teachers saw her talent. The teacher encouraged Cisneros to join the school literary magazine. She also had Cisneros read her poems in class.

After high school, Cisneros went to Loyola University in Chicago. She majored in English. She began to think about a career as a writer. Cisneros's mother supported her career goals. But her father thought that a woman did not need a career. He believed that her job was to be a mother and a wife. His ideas created tension between Cisneros and him.

After she graduated from college, Cisneros enrolled in the University of Iowa Writers' Workshop. This famous writing program helps talented writers develop their skill. Few of the other students came from poor families. And Cisneros was the only Chicano. At first she felt uncomfortable and separate. But in time, her experiences became her inspiration. She said, "I decided I would write about something my classmates couldn't write about."[2] She wanted to tell stories that were never told before.

Cisneros wrote stories about the people she observed in the barrio—the Hispanic neighborhood. The stories were sometimes funny and sometimes touching. But they were always realistic. She wrote about how Latino culture empowered men. And she showed how barrio life took power away from women. Men made the rules. Women didn't control their own lives. They grew up in the barrio, lived there, and died there. They never left. Cisneros combined these stories into a book called *The House on Mango Street.*

Cisneros used a young female narrator to tell the stories. Her name was Esperanza. In Spanish, *esperanza* means "hope." In the book, Esperanza matures. At the end, she tells about her plans to leave the barrio. She wants her own separate identity. She wants to be equal to men. She says, "I have begun my own quiet war. Simple. Sure. I am one who leaves the table like a man, without putting back the chair or picking up the plate."[3]

At first, Cisneros worried that her book betrayed her Chicano culture. She told the world stories that only Chicanos knew. But her book became popular. It sold more than half a million copies. It is now used in schools from middle schools through universities.

After the success of *The House on Mango Street,* Cisneros received many grants. These grants supported her while she was writing. She published a book of poetry, *My Wicked, Wicked Ways,* in 1987.

Then in 1991, Cisneros published *Woman Hollering Creek and Other Stories.* In this book, Cisneros shows Chicano life on the Mexico/Texas border. She uses a strong feminist voice. She shows powerful women. She expresses her belief in the equality of men and women.

In 1994, she followed with another book of poetry called *Loose Woman.* And in 2002, she published *Caramelo, or, Puro Cuento: A Novel.*

Recently, Cisneros's father finally read some of his daughter's work. He read it in Spanish. He now recognizes her talent. Cisneros feels that they have made peace with one another.

Cisneros currently lives and writes in San Antonio, Texas.

In 1995, Sandra Cisneros received a MacArthur Foundation grant. The MacArthur Foundation gives large grants to creative people. Because the grants honor the brightest, most talented people, they are sometimes called "genius grants."

Comprehension

Complete the sentences. Use information from the reading.

1. Because Cisneros didn't like moving often, _____

   _____

   _____.

2. In high school, Cisneros became more confident in her writing when _____

   _____

   _____.

3. There was tension between Cisneros and her father because _____

   _____

   _____.

4. At the University of Iowa Writers' Workshop, Cisneros decided _____

   _____

   _____.

5. Cisneros's stories are about _____

   _____

   _____.

6. At the end of *The House on Mango Street*, Esperanza plans _____

   _____

   _____.

7. After reading some of his daughter's work, Cisneros's father _____

   _____

   _____.

Fact or Opinion

Work with a partner. Decide if each sentence is a fact or an opinion.
Then write *F* for *fact* or *O* for *opinion* in front of each sentence.

_____ 1. It's good that Cisneros made peace with her father.

_____ 2. As a child, Cisneros read many books.

_____ 3. Cisneros found inspiration at the University of
Iowa Writers' Workshop.

_____ 4. Cultural pride was important in the Chicano movement.

Vocabulary

Look at these words from the reading. Put a check next to words that
you know. Underline words that you don't know yet. Find the words in
the reading. Try to guess their meanings.

| betray | empower | inspiration | literary |
| emerge | feminist | introverted | touching |

Match each word with its definition.

_____ 1. emerge   a. to give control or authority to

_____ 2. introverted   b. to appear

_____ 3. literary   c. emotionally moving

_____ 4. inspiration   d. related to literature

_____ 5. touching   e. to be disloyal to; to give away a secret

_____ 6. empower   f. shy

_____ 7. betray   g. a source of ideas

_____ 8. feminist   h. person who believes that men and women are equal

Reading a Chart

A chart is a useful way to organize facts.

Important Chicano Writers

Writer	Type of writing	Other information
Luis Valdez	plays	He began El Teatro Campesino (The Farmworkers' Theater) in 1965. In 1978, he wrote *Zoot Suit*. In 1979, it became the first Chicano play on Broadway.
Denise Chávez	novels short stories plays children's books	Her novel *Face of an Angel* won several awards in 1995. One of them was the American Book Award.
Rudolfo Anaya	novels	He was one of the first writers of the Chicano movement. His 1972 book, *Bless Me Ultima*, has sold more than 360,000 copies.
Gary Soto	poetry novels children's books	He has published many books of poetry. He has also won many awards. He received two grants from the National Endowment for the Arts.

Fill in the blanks. Use information from the chart.

1. _____ and _____ write books for children.

2. Rudolfo Anaya's best-known book is _____.

3. _____ wrote plays for farm workers.

4. Luis Valdez wrote a Broadway play called _____.

5. _____ won two National Endowment for the Arts grants.

6. Gary Soto writes novels and _____.

7. _____ was one of the first writers of the Chicano movement.

8. The novel _____ won the American Book Award.

Connecting Today and Yesterday

1. The Chicano movement used different art forms to show cultural pride. These art forms included writing, dance, theater, and painting. Do other ethnic groups today show cultural pride with art? If yes, which groups? How do they show pride in their culture?

2. Cisneros believes that Chicano culture values women less than men. Are women's roles valued as highly as men's in other cultures in the United States? Explain.

Group Activity

Research the Chicano movement in the United States. Bring information to class. In your group, discuss these questions.

1. Who led the Chicano movement? Were they men and women?

2. How did the movement improve job opportunities for Chicanos? For others?

3. How did the movement improve education for Chicanos? For others?

Class Discussion

1. Cisneros and her father expected different things for her life. Cisneros followed her own path. In a conflict like this one, should children follow their own ideas or their parents' ideas? Explain.

2. Cisneros writes about living in two cultures at once. Have you ever lived like this? If yes, what problems did it create?

3. Cisneros worried that she betrayed her culture. What do you think? Is it right to show others negative parts of your culture? Explain.

Reflections

1. What was the most interesting thing that you read in this lesson?

2. Can you use anything from Sandra Cisneros's story in your own life? Explain.

In *The House on Mango Street*, Esperanza says, "One day I'll have my own house, but I won't forget who I am or where I came from."[4]

What does she mean?

Bruce Lee

"One must always strive to be better. The sky's the limit!"
—Bruce Lee[1]

Pre-Reading Questions

1. Read the words under the title. What do you think that they mean?

2. Is it important to improve yourself? Explain your opinion.

Reading Preview

Bruce Lee was a popular martial artist and film star. He developed his own style of martial arts. He helped make martial arts popular in the United States. And he opened the door for more Asian American film actors.

Bruce Lee

At one time, U.S. films showed Asians only as servants or lowly laborers. There were no Asian American movie stars. Sometimes filmmakers wouldn't hire Asian actors for Asian roles. Instead, they used makeup to make Caucasians look Asian. But in the 1970s, Bruce Lee and his films helped change this.

Bruce Lee was born in San Francisco on November 27, 1940. His father was a Hong Kong opera singer who was on tour. Lee was a sickly child. His mother worried about his health, and she was superstitious. She gave him a special Chinese name to protect him from bad luck.

When Lee was still a baby, the family returned to Hong Kong. There, he became a celebrity at an early age. He was a child movie star. By the time he was 18 years old, he had been in 20 movies. Lee had little interest in school. He spent his time with street gangs.

When he was a teenager, Lee took his first martial arts class. He studied the style of kung fu called Wing Chu. He had great athletic ability, and he learned quickly. In 1958, he entered the Hong Kong interscholastic boxing championships. He easily defeated the champion of the past three years.

In 1959, Lee got in trouble for fighting. So his parents sent him to live with a friend near Seattle, Washington. He worked at the friend's restaurant. While he was in Washington, Lee finished high school. Next, he enrolled at the University of Washington. He became a philosophy major. He also taught martial arts classes. While he was teaching, he met his future wife, Linda Emery. They married in 1964.

Soon Lee opened his own martial arts school in Seattle. He began to formulate his own style of martial arts. He called it Jeet Kune Do. He believed that other forms of martial arts were too mechanical. Lee developed techniques that allowed a person to react quickly and realistically. His style used rapid-fire kicks and punches.

Lee believed that martial arts were a form of self-expression. He combined elements of U.S. individuality with ancient martial arts techniques. He wanted to share Eastern culture with the West. In the past, few people in the United States learned kung fu techniques.

In 1964, Lee competed in an international karate championship in Long Beach, California. He dazzled the audience. They were amazed at his speed and precision. As a result, Lee was offered a role in the TV series *The Green Hornet.* Lee played the hero's sidekick, Kato. Kato used martial arts to fight crime. Lee gained some recognition in this role. But as an Asian American, he found it hard to get other good roles.

He returned to Hong Kong in 1971. There he starred in two martial arts films: *Fists of Fury* and *The Chinese Connection.* These films made him a major star in Asia. In them, he demonstrated strength and invincibility. And his martial arts sequences were exciting. In one film, Lee's flying kick was so fast that it looked like trick photography.

In 1973, Lee starred in his first major Hollywood action film. It was called *Enter the Dragon.* Toward the end of production, Lee collapsed. He recovered. But five weeks later, he died suddenly in Hong Kong. The coroner said that swelling of the brain killed him.

This explanation didn't satisfy some of Lee's fans. They still argue about the cause of his death. Some claim that he was murdered. Others say that he was cursed. In 1993, a movie was made about Lee's life. It was called *Dragon: The Bruce Lee Story.*

Lee combined Eastern and Western philosophies in his work and his life. He helped to create a new kind of movie hero. And he opened the door for more Asian Americans in U.S. films.

Comprehension

Check the correct answer.

1. Lee and his work

_____ a. did not change the image of Asians in U.S. films.

_____ b. created a new image of Asians in U.S. films.

2. Lee's mother gave him a special name

_____ a. to protect him from bad luck.

_____ b. because she wanted him to be a hero.

3. Lee had his first martial arts class

_____ a. when he was a young child.

_____ b. when he was a teenager.

4. Lee's martial arts system

_____ a. used quick kicks and punches.

_____ b. followed traditional techniques.

5. Lee first impressed a U.S. audience

_____ a. at the international karate championship in Long Beach.

_____ b. when he played Kato in *The Green Hornet*.

6. *Enter the Dragon*

_____ a. was Lee's first U.S. film.

_____ b. was not popular.

7. Lee's life and work

_____ a. combined ideas from Eastern and Western culture.

_____ b. used mainly ideas from Eastern culture.

Bruce Lee spent six days a week practicing. He said, "I trained my hands every Monday, Wednesday, and Friday. I trained my legs on alternate days."[2]

Sequence

Work with a partner. Number the events in the correct order.

_____ Lee opens his own martial arts studio.

_____ Lee plays Kato in *The Green Hornet*.

_____ Lee wins the Hong Kong interscholastic boxing championships.

_____ Lee films *Enter the Dragon*.

_____ Lee goes to Washington University.

Vocabulary

Look at these words from the reading. Put a check next to words that you know. Underline words that you don't know yet. Find the words in the reading. Try to guess their meanings.

celebrity	formulate	lowly	precision
dazzled	invincibility	mechanical	superstitious

Use the words to fill in the blanks in the sentences.

1. Humble people who are not important are _____.

2. Lee's mother was _____ and worried about bad luck.

3. A _____ is a famous person.

4. Lee began to _____, or put together, his own martial arts system.

5. A movement that is _____ doesn't look natural.

6. Lee's quick kicks and punches _____ the audience.

7. When something is done with _____, everything is exactly right.

8. In his films, Lee showed _____ when he could not be defeated.

Reading a Time Line

A time line shows dates and events in order on a line.

Bruce Lee's Life

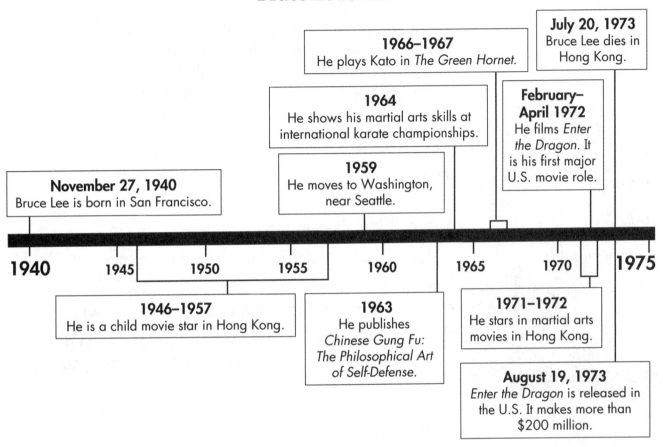

Answer the questions. Use information from the time line.

1. How many years was Lee a child movie star? _____

2. How old was Lee when he published *Chinese Gung Fu?* _____

3. How long did Lee work on *The Green Hornet?* _____

4. How long did Lee work on filming *Enter the Dragon?* _____

5. How old was Lee when he died? _____

Bruce Lee said, "Research your own experiences for the truth . . . . The creating individual . . . is more important than any style or system."[3]

What did he mean?

Connecting Today and Yesterday

1. Lee was popular in both Eastern and Western cultures. Do any celebrities today unite two cultures? If yes, who? Why is the person popular?

2. Lee, an Asian, married Linda Emery, a Caucasian. Emery's mother worried that other people would not accept an interracial marriage. Why were interracial marriages controversial? Are they accepted today?

Group Activities

1. Lee's mother was superstitious. In your group, make a list of superstitions. Then answer these questions:

   - Are any of the superstitions true?
   - Are any of the superstitions the same in different cultures?
   - Are superstitions powerful in society? If yes, why?

2. Watch the film *Dragon: The Bruce Lee Story*. Then discuss it in your group. What surprised you? What did you learn about Lee?

Class Discussion

1. Some martial arts films used trick photography. Lee never did this. What does this show about his personality?

2. Martial arts films contain violence. Are these movies good for children? Why or why not?

3. How were Jackie Robinson and Bruce Lee alike? How were they different?

Reflections

1. What was the most interesting thing you read in this lesson?

2. What can you do to learn more about Bruce Lee or martial arts?

Notes and References

General References

Columbia Encyclopedia, 6th ed. New York: Columbia University Press, 2000.

Morison, Samuel Eliot; Henry Steele Commager; and William E. Leuchtenburg. *A Concise History of the American Republic*, 2nd ed. New York: Oxford University Press, 1983.

Rice, Arnold M.; John A. Krout; and Charles M. Harris. *United States History to 1877*. New York: Harper Perennial, 1991.

The Time 100: The Most Important People of the Century, 1999. Online at www.time.com/time/time100 (retrieved July 22, 2004).

World Book Online Reference Center. World Book, Inc., 2004. www.worldbookonline.com (retrieved July 22, 2004).

Anne Bradstreet

Notes

1. Anne Bradstreet, "Meditations, Divine and Morall," 1664, quoted in chapter XIV of Campbell, *Anne Bradstreet and Her Time*.

2. Anne Bradstreet, "Another II," in *Several Poems*, Boston: John Foster, 1678.

3. Anne Bradstreet, "Another," in *Several Poems*, Boston: John Foster, 1678.

4. Quoted in Martin, *An American Triptych*, p. 19.

References

Campbell, Helen. *Anne Bradstreet and Her Time*. Boston: Lothrop, 1891.

Cowell, Pattie. "Anne Bradstreet (1612?–1672)." On the web site of Randy Bass, English Department, Georgetown University, www.georgetown.edu/faculty/bassr/heath/syllabuild/iguide/bradstre.html (retrieved July 21, 2004).

Hensley, Jeannine, ed. *The Works of Anne Bradstreet*. Belknap Press, 1967.

Martin, Wendy. *An American Triptych: Anne Bradstreet, Emily Dickinson, Adrienne Rich*. Chapel Hill: University of North Carolina Press, 1984.

Woodlief, Ann. "Anne Bradstreet: Biography." On the web site of the English Department, Virginia Commonwealth University, www.vcu.edu/engweb/eng384/bradbio.htm (retrieved July 21, 2004).

Samuel Adams

Notes

1. from "Ballad of the Tea Party," in Burl Ives and Albert Hague, *The Burl Ives Song Book*, New York: Ballantine Books, 1953.

2. Samuel Adams, "American Independence," speech given Aug. 1, 1776, text on the web site of the Douglass Archives of American Public Address, douglassarchives.org/adam_a29.htm (retrieved July 16, 2004).

References

Brody, Seymour. "Haym Salomon: Financier of the Revolutionary War," in *Jewish Heroes and Heroines in America from Colonial Times to 1900*. Hollywood, FL: Lifetime Books, 1996.

"December 16, 1773," 2000. On the web site of the Boston Tea Party Ship and Museum, www.bostonteapartyship.com (retrieved July 22, 2004).

Eddlem, Thomas R. "Father of the American Revolution." *The New American*, July 29, 2002, vol. 18, issue 15, pp. 33–38.

Hosmer, James K. *Samuel Adams*. New York: The Riverside Press, 1888.

Hoyle, John Christian. "Paul Revere's Ride." *Christian Science Monitor*, April 14, 1998, vol. 90, issue 96, p. 8.

Middlekauff, Robert. *The Glorious Cause: The American Revolution, 1763–1789*. New York: Oxford University Press, 1985.

National Statuary Hall Collection, Office of the Curator. "Samuel Adams," 2003. On the web site of the Architect of the Capitol, www.aoc.gov/cc/art/nsh/adams.htm (retrieved July 22, 2004).

Public Broadcasting Service. Web site for *Liberty! The American Revolution*, www.pbs.org/ktca/liberty/ (retrieved July 22, 2004).

Benjamin Franklin

Notes

1. Benjamin Franklin, *Poor Richard's Almanac*, 1757, cited in "Benjamin Franklin (1706–1790)," John Bartlett, comp., *Familiar Quotations*, 10th ed., 1919.

2. Benjamin Franklin, from *Respectfully Quoted: A Dictionary of Quotations Requested from the Congressional Research Service*, Washington, D.C.: Library of Congress, 1989.

3. Ellen Hovde, quoted in Mary Lou Beatty, "A Time Full of Shadows." *Humanities*, July/August 2002, vol. 23, no. 4.

4. John Adams, *John Adams Autobiography*, part 2, "Travels and Negotiations," 1777–1778, original manuscript from the Adams Family Papers, Massachusetts Historical Society.

References

"The Amazing Adventures of Benjamin Franklin." *Time Online Edition*, www.time.com/time/2003/franklin/ (retrieved July 23, 2004).

"American Electric." *The New Yorker*, June 30, 2003.

"Benjamin Franklin: Glimpses of the Man," 1994. On the web site *Franklin Institute Online*, sln.fi.edu/franklin (retrieved July 27, 2004).

Public Broadcasting Service. Web site for *Benjamin Franklin*, www.pbs.org/benfranklin/ (retrieved July 27, 2004).

Sacagawea

Notes

1. Erica Funkhouser, in an interview on *Lewis and Clark: The Journey of the Corps of Discovery*, text on www.pbs.org/lewisandclark/living/idx_4.html (retrieved Aug. 12, 2004).

2. William Least Heat-Moon, in an interview on *Lewis and Clark: The Journey of the Corps of Discovery*, text on www.pbs.org/lewisandclark/living/idx_4.html (retrieved Aug. 12, 2004).

3. McBeth, "Sacagawea."

References

Ambrose, Stephen. *Undaunted Courage: Meriwether Lewis, Thomas Jefferson, and the Opening of the American West.* New York: Simon and Schuster, 1996.

McBeth, Sally. "Sacagawea," in *Encyclopedia of North American Indians.* Boston: Houghton Mifflin, 1996.

National Park Service. *Lewis and Clark Expedition.* Online at www.cr.nps.gov/nr/travel/lewisandclark/index.htm (retrieved July 27, 2004).

Public Broadcasting Service. Web site for *Lewis and Clark: The Journey of the Corps of Discovery, A Film by Ken Burns,* 1997. PBS Online, www.pbs.org/lewisandclark (retrieved July 16, 2004).

Public Broadcasting Service. "Sacagawea." On the web site for *New Perspectives on the West,* www.pbs.org/weta/thewest/people/s_z/sacagawea.htm (retrieved July 23, 2004).

"Searching for Sacagawea," *National Geographic,* Feb. 2003.

U.S. Mint. "Golden Dollar Coin." Online at www.usmint.gov/mint_programs/index.cfm?action=golden_dollar_coin (retrieved July 27, 2004).

Abraham Lincoln

Notes

1. Abraham Lincoln, from the speech "A House Divided" at Springfield, Illinois, June 16, 1858, in *Collected Works of Abraham Lincoln,* vol. 2, p. 461, Rutgers University Press, 1990, cited in *The Columbia World of Quotations,* New York: Columbia University Press, 1996.

2. Public Broadcasting Service, fact sheet on the web site for *The Civil War, A Film by Ken Burns,* 1990, www.pbs.org/civilwar/war/facts.html (retrieved July 20, 2004).

3. Figures from Nofi, "Statistical Summary: America's Major Wars."

References

Nofi, Al. "Statistical Summary: America's Major Wars," 2001. On the web site of The United States Civil War Center, www.cwc.lsu.edu/cwc/other/stats/warcost.htm (retrieved July 27, 2004).

Public Broadcasting Service. Transcript of interview with David Herbert Donald, "Lincoln: A New Biography. Text online at www.pbs.org/newshour/gergen/donald.html (retrieved July 27, 2004).

Public Broadcasting Service. Web site of *Freedom: A History of US.* www.pbs.org/wnet/historyofus/ (retrieved July 27, 2004).

Public Broadcasting Service. "Abraham Lincoln." On the web site of *American Experience,* www.pbs.org/wgbh/amex/presidents/16_lincoln/ (retrieved July 27, 2004).

Public Broadcasting Service. "The Time of the Lincolns." On the web site of *American Experience,* www.pbs.org/wgbh/amex/lincolns/ (retrieved July 27, 2004).

Public Broadcasting Service. "Who Is Abraham Lincoln?" Transcript from *Think Tank with Ben Wattenberg,* text online at www.pbs.org/thinktank/transcript247.html (retrieved July 27, 2004).

Harriet Tubman

Notes

1. Harriet Tubman, quoted in Sarah Bradford, *Harriet, the Moses of Her People,* 1869, cited in *The Columbia World of Quotations,* New York: Columbia University Press, 1996.

2. Webster, "Traveling the Long Road to Freedom."

3. Tobin and Dobard, *Hidden in Plain View.*

4. Harriet Tubman, quoted in Lyde Cullen Sizer, *Divided Houses,* ch. 7, 1992, cited in *The Columbia World of Quotations,* New York: Columbia University Press, 1996.

References

Lewis, Jone Johnson. "Harriet Tubman—Moses of Her People." *Women's History Guide* at womenshistory.about.com/library/weekly/aa020419a.htm (retrieved Aug. 4, 2004).

"The Life of Harriet Tubman." On the web site of New York History Net, www.nyhistory.com/harriettubman/life.htm (retrieved July 23, 2004).

Litwack, Leon; and August Meier. *Black Leaders of the Nineteenth Century.* Urbana: University of Illinois Press, 1988.

Tobin, Jacqueline L.; and Raymond G. Dobard. *Hidden in Plain View: A Secret Story of Quilts and the Underground Railroad.* New York: Anchor Books, 2000.

Webster, Donovan. "Traveling the Long Road to Freedom, One Step at a Time." *Smithsonian,* Oct. 1996, Vol. 27, Issue 7, p. 48.

Mark Twain

Notes

1. Mark Twain, quoted on Public Broadcasting Service, web site for *Mark Twain,* www.pbs.org/marktwain/learnmore/activities.html (retrieved Aug. 12, 2004).

2. Mark Twain, quoted on Public Broadcasting Service, web site for *Mark Twain,* www.pbs.org/marktwain/scrapbook/09_mysterious_stranger/index.html (retrieved Aug. 12, 2004).

3. Ernest Hemingway, *The Green Hills of Africa,* ch. 1 (1935), cited in *The Columbia World of Quotations,* New York: Columbia University Press, 1996.

4. Mark Twain, "More Maxims of Mark," *Mark Twain: Collected Tales, Sketches, Speeches, & Essays, 1891–1910,* Library of America, 1992, p. 943, cited in *The Columbia World of Quotations,* New York: Columbia University Press, 1996.

5. Mark Twain, *North American Review,* vol. 184, no. 606, Jan. 4, 1907, cited in *The Columbia World of Quotations,* New York: Columbia University Press, 1996.

References

Public Broadcasting Service. Web site for *Mark Twain,* www.pbs.org/marktwain/ (retrieved July 28, 2004).

Public Broadcasting Service. Web site for *New Perspectives on the West,* 1996. Online at www.pbs.org/weta/thewest (retrieved July 28, 2004).

Schmitt, Barbara. *Mark Twain Quotations, Newspaper Collections, & Related Resources.* Online at Twainquotes.com/index.html (retrieved July 28, 2004).

Theodore Roosevelt

Notes

1. Theodore Roosevelt, from a speech on April 2, 1903, Chicago, *The Works of Theodore Roosevelt,* vol. 13, cited in *The Columbia World of Quotations,* New York: Columbia University Press, 1996.

2. Theodore Roosevelt, quoted by David McCullough in an interview on "TR: The Story of Theodore Roosevelt," text at www.pbs.org/wgbh/amex/tr/mccull4.html (retrieved Aug. 12, 2004).

References

Hanson, David C. "Theodore Roosevelt and the Panama Canal." On the web site of Virginia Western Community College, www.vw.cc.va.us/vwhansd/HIS122/Teddy/TRCanal.html (retrieved July 28, 2004).

Library of Congress, "Progressive Era (1890–1913)." In *America's Story from America's Library*, www.americaslibrary.gov/cgi-bin/page.cgi/jb/progress (retrieved July 27, 2004).

Public Broadcasting Service. Web site for "TR: The Story of Theodore Roosevelt," *American Experience*, 1996. Text at PBS Online, www.pbs.org/wgbh/amex/tr (retrieved July 28, 2004).

Theodore Roosevelt Association. Web site. Online at www.theodoreroosevelt.org (retrieved July 23, 2004).

Emma Lazarus

Notes

1. Emma Lazarus, "The New Colossus," ln. 14, in *America in Poetry*. Charles Sullivan, ed., 1988, Harry N. Abrams, cited in *The Columbia World of Quotations*, New York: Columbia University Press, 1996.
2. *Illustrated London News*, quoted in "Emma Lazarus, 1849–1887," on the web site of the Jewish Women's Archive, www.jwa.org/exhibits/wov/lazarus/el5.html (retrieved Aug. 12, 2004).
3. *The Critic*, quoted in "Emma Lazarus, 1849–1887," on the web site of the Jewish Women's Archive, www.jwa.org/exhibits/wov/lazarus/el5.html (retrieved Aug. 12, 2004).
4. "Visiting the Statue of Liberty and Ellis Island Immigration Museum," on the web site of the Ellis Island Immigration Museum, www.ellisisland.com/indexInfo.html (retrieved Aug. 5, 2004).
5. U.S. Bureau of the Census, *Historical Statistics of the United States, Colonial Times to 1970*, Bicentennial Edition. Washington, D.C., 1975.

References

Adler, Cyrus; and Henrietta Szold. "Lazarus, Emma." *JewishEncyclopedia.com*, jewishencyclopedia.com/view.jsp?artid=119&letter=L&search=Emma%20Lazarus (retrieved July 28, 2004).

"Emma Lazarus, 1849–1887." On the web site of the Jewish Women's Archive, www.jwa.org/exhibits/wov/lazarus/el1.html (retrieved Aug. 5, 2004).

Public Broadcasting Service. Web site for *The Statue of Liberty*, 1985. Text at PBS Online, www.pbs.org/kenburns/statueofliberty (retrieved July 29, 2004).

U.S. Bureau of the Census. *Historical Statistics of the United States, Colonial Times to 1970*, Bicentennial Edition. Washington, D.C., 1975.

Woody Guthrie

Notes

1. Woody Guthrie, letter to Alan Lomax, Sept. 19, 1940, image online on the Library of Congress

American Memory web site, memory.loc.gov/cgi-bin/ampage?collId=afcwwg&fileName=004/004page.db&itemLink=D?afcwwgbib:3:./temp/~ammem_UJyq:: (retrieved Aug. 5, 2004).
2. Woody Guthrie, letter to Alan Lomax, Sept. 19, 1940, image online on the Library of Congress *American Memory* web site, memory.loc.gov/cgi-bin/query/D?afcwwgbib:3:./temp/~ammem_Po8D:: (retrieved Aug. 5, 2004).
3. Klein, *Woody Guthrie, A Life*, p. 160.

References

Klein, Joe. *Woody Guthrie, A Life*. New York: Alfred A, Knopf, 1980.

Library of Congress. *American Memory* web site. Online at lcweb2.loc.gov/ammem (retrieved July 29, 2004).

National Park Service. Web site of the Route 66 Corridor Preservation Program. www.cr.nps.gov/rt66/ (retrieved July 29, 2004).

Public Broadcasting Service. "Mass Exodus from the Plains." On the web site of "Surviving the Dust Bowl," *American Experience*, Public Broadcasting Service, www.pbs.org/wgbh/amex/dustbowl/peopleevents/pandeAMEX08.html (retrieved May 25, 2004).

Helen Keller

Notes

1. Helen Keller, inscription in autograph album of Lafayette E. Cornwell, Yonkers, New York, quoted in Walter Fogg, *One Thousand Sayings of History*, 1929, p. 17, cited in *The Columbia World of Quotations*, New York: Columbia University Press, 1996.
2. Mark Twain, quoted in American Foundation for the Blind, "The Life of Helen Keller," at www.afb.org/Section.asp?DocumentID=1351 (retrieved July 21, 2004).
3. American Foundation for the Blind, "Helen Keller: An Overview," at www.afb.org/Section.asp?SectionID=1&TopicID=129 (retrieved Aug. 4, 2004).
4. Helen Keller, "Three Days to See," *Atlantic Monthly*, Jan. 1933, text at the web site of the American Foundation for the Blind, www.afb.org/Section.asp?DocumentID+1215 (retrieved July 21, 2004).

References

American Foundation for the Blind. "Chronology of Helen Keller's Life." From *To Love This Life: Quotations by Helen Keller*. New York: AFB Press, 2000. Text online at www.afb.org/section.asp?Documentid=1353 (retrieved July 29, 2004).

Hermann, Dorothy. *Helen Keller, A Life*. New York: Alfred A. Knopf, 1998.

Royal National Institute of the Blind. "The Life of Helen Keller." Text online at www.rnib.org.uk/xpedio/groups/public/documents/publicwebsite/public_keller.hcsp (retrieved July 29, 2004).

Jackie Robinson

Notes

1. Henry Aaron, "Jackie Robinson," in *The Time 100: The Most Important People of the Century*, 1999, text at www.time.com/time/time100/heroes/profile/robinson02.html (retrieved Aug. 2, 2004).

2. Roger Wilkins in "Jackie Robinson: Historians," text at www.pbs.org/newshour/bb/sports/hist_4-15.html (retrieved Aug. 2, 2004).
3. National Baseball Hall of Fame and Museum web site, www.baseballhalloffame.org (retrieved Aug. 6, 2004).
4. Charles Barkley, quoted in Lopez, "He Did It for a Greater Good."

References

"Jackie Robinson: Historians." Transcript of segment of *The NewsHour with Jim Lehrer*, broadcast April 15, 1997. Text online at www.pbs.org/newshour/bb/sports/hist_4-15.html (retrieved Aug. 2, 2004).

"Jackie Robinson." *Current Biography*. Feb. 1947, pp. 544–547.

Lopez, John P. "He Did It for a Greater Good." *Houston Chronicle*, undated. Text at www.chron.com/content/chronicle/sports/special/barriers/history.html (retrieved July 21, 2004).

Public Broadcasting Service. Web site for *Baseball, A Film by Ken Burns*, 1994. Text at PBS Online, www.pbs.org/kenburns/baseball (retrieved Aug. 5, 2004).

Rust, Art and Edna Rust. *Art Rust's Illustrated History of the Black Athlete*. Garden City, NY: Doubleday, 1985.

John F. Kennedy

Notes

1. Kennedy, *Profiles in Courage*, p. 246.
2. John F. Kennedy, Civil Rights Announcement, June 11, 1963, text at www.pbs.org/wgbh/amex/presidents/35_kennedy/psources/ps_civilrights.html (retrieved Aug. 3, 2004).
3. John F. Kennedy, Inaugural Address, Washington, D.C., Jan. 20, 1961, text on the web site of John F. Kennedy Library and Museum, www.jfklibrary.org/j012061.htm (retrieved July 21, 2004).

References

Kennedy, John F. *Profiles in Courage*. New York: Harper & Bros., 1956.

Public Broadcasting Service. Web site for "The Kennedys," *American Experience*, 1996. Text at PBS Online, www.pbs.org/wgbh/amex/kennedys (retrieved Aug. 5, 2004).

Web site of the John F. Kennedy Library and Museum, www.jfklibrary.org (retrieved Aug. 3, 2004).

Sandra Cisneros

Notes

1. Sandra Cisneros, author description for *The House on Mango Street*, on the Random House web site at www.randomhouse.com/acmart/catalog/display.pperl?isbn=0679734775&view=amauthbio (retrieved Aug. 5, 2004).
2. Sandra Cisneros, quoted in Jim Sagel, "Sandra Cisneros: Conveying the Riches of the Latin American Culture Is the Author's Literary Goal," *Publisher's Weekly*, March 29, 1991, text at www.lasmujeres.com/sandracisneros/cisnerosgoal2.shtml (retrieved July 22, 2004).
3. Cisneros, *The House on Mango Street*.
4. Cisneros, *The House on Mango Street*.

References

California Department of Parks and Recreation, Office of Historic Preservation. "A History of Mexican Americans in California." in *Five Views: An Ethnic Historic Site Survey for California*, 1988. On the National Park Service web site, www.cr.nps.gov/history/online_books/5views/5views5e.htm (retrieved Aug. 5, 2004).

Chavez, Andres. "Sandra Cisneros." In Diane Telgen and Jim Kamp, eds. *Notable Hispanic American Women*. Farmington Hills, MI Gale Group, 1993.

Cisneros, Sandra. *The House on Mango Street*. New York: Vintage Books, 1991.

"Denise Chávez," 1996. On the web site of the School of Humanities Visiting Poets and Writers Series, St. Edward's University, Austin, TX, www.stedwards.edu/hum/drummond/chavez.html (retrieved Aug. 5, 2004)

Lowry, Kathy. "The Purple Passion of Sandra Cisneros." *Texas Monthly*, Oct. 1997, vol. 25, issue 10.

"The MacArthur Fellows Program: Overview." On the web site of the MacArthur Foundation, www.macfdn.org/programs/fel/fel_overview.htm (retrieved Aug. 5, 2004).

"Official Gary Soto Website," garysoto.com (retrieved Aug. 5, 2004).

"Rudolfo Anaya." On the web site for the public radio series *Writing the Southwest*, www.unm.edu/~wrtgsw/anaya.html (retrieved Aug. 5, 2004).

Satz, Martha. "Returning to One's House." *Southwest Review*, Spring 1997, vol. 82, issue 2, p. 166.

Bruce Lee

Notes

1. Lee, *Words of the Dragon*, p. 142.
2. Lee, *Words of the Dragon*, p. 123.
3. Bruce Lee, quoted in Joel Stein, "Bruce Lee," in *The Time 100: The Most Important People of the Century*, 1999, text at www.time.com/time/time100/heroes/profile/lee03.html (retrieved July 22, 2004).

References

"Bruce Lee Still Kicks High," CBS News: Entertainment, July 18, 2003. Text at www.cbsnews.com/stories/2003/07/18/entertainment/main564038.shtml (retrieved Aug. 5, 2004).

Lee, Bruce. *Words of the Dragon: Interviews, 1958–1973*, John Little, ed. Boston: Tuttle Publishing, 1997.

Yuan, Shu. "From Bruce Lee to Jackie Chan." *Journal of Popular Film and Television*. Summer 2003, vol. 31, issue 2, p. 250.